D1604834

Afghan Sentiments™

the Needlecraft Shop™

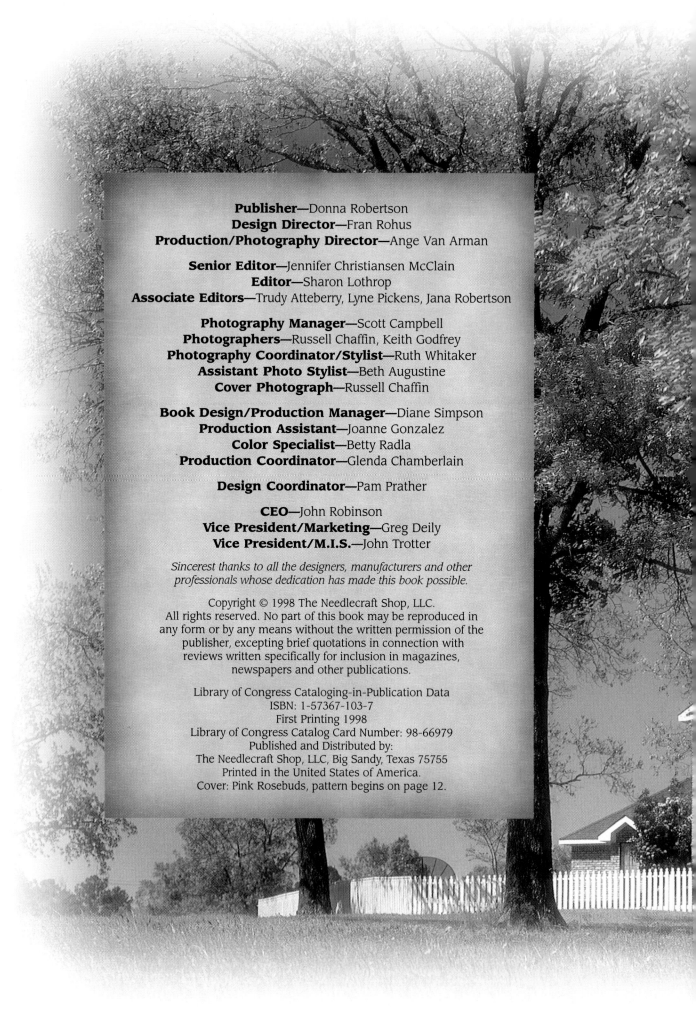

Publisher—Donna Robertson
Design Director—Fran Rohus
Production/Photography Director—Ange Van Arman

Senior Editor—Jennifer Christiansen McClain
Editor—Sharon Lothrop
Associate Editors—Trudy Atteberry, Lyne Pickens, Jana Robertson

Photography Manager—Scott Campbell
Photographers—Russell Chaffin, Keith Godfrey
Photography Coordinator/Stylist—Ruth Whitaker
Assistant Photo Stylist—Beth Augustine
Cover Photograph—Russell Chaffin

Book Design/Production Manager—Diane Simpson
Production Assistant—Joanne Gonzalez
Color Specialist—Betty Radla
Production Coordinator—Glenda Chamberlain

Design Coordinator—Pam Prather

CEO—John Robinson
Vice President/Marketing—Greg Deily
Vice President/M.I.S.—John Trotter

*Sincerest thanks to all the designers, manufacturers and other
professionals whose dedication has made this book possible.*

Copyright © 1998 The Needlecraft Shop, LLC.
All rights reserved. No part of this book may be reproduced in
any form or by any means without the written permission of the
publisher, excepting brief quotations in connection with
reviews written specifically for inclusion in magazines,
newspapers and other publications.

Library of Congress Cataloging-in-Publication Data
ISBN: 1-57367-103-7
First Printing 1998
Library of Congress Catalog Card Number: 98-66979
Published and Distributed by:
The Needlecraft Shop, LLC, Big Sandy, Texas 75755
Printed in the United States of America.
Cover: Pink Rosebuds, pattern begins on page 12.

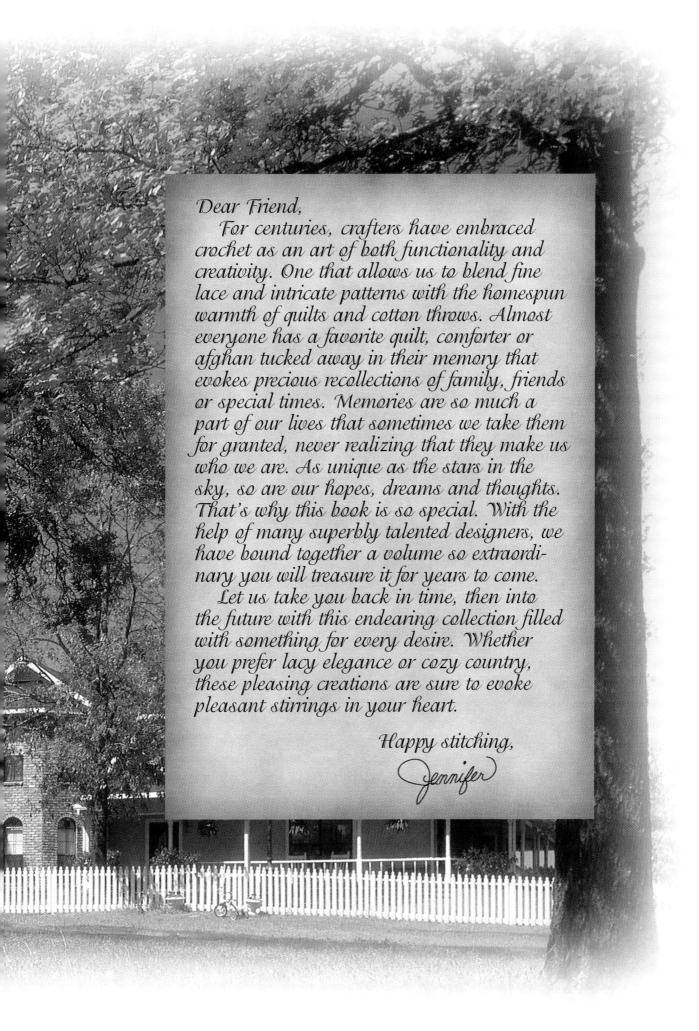

Dear Friend,

For centuries, crafters have embraced crochet as an art of both functionality and creativity. One that allows us to blend fine lace and intricate patterns with the homespun warmth of quilts and cotton throws. Almost everyone has a favorite quilt, comforter or afghan tucked away in their memory that evokes precious recollections of family, friends or special times. Memories are so much a part of our lives that sometimes we take them for granted, never realizing that they make us who we are. As unique as the stars in the sky, so are our hopes, dreams and thoughts. That's why this book is so special. With the help of many superbly talented designers, we have bound together a volume so extraordinary you will treasure it for years to come.

Let us take you back in time, then into the future with this endearing collection filled with something for every desire. Whether you prefer lacy elegance or cozy country, these pleasing creations are sure to evoke pleasant stirrings in your heart.

Happy stitching,

Jennifer

Contents

Legends

Tidings

Romantics

Bouquets

As innocent as a child's dreams, the perineal beauty of flowers bespeaks eternal youth, captured forever in the form of velvety petals. An ever-blooming bounty of dazzling blooms, these resplendent designs will brighten your soul with the radiance only nature can provide. Come stroll through the garden and relax a while, then stitch your own private collection of crochet hybrids.

Flower Garden

Designed by Beverly Mewhorter

Finished Size: 46" x 56" not including Fringe.

Materials: Worsted-weight yarn — 14 oz. each dk. green, med. green and lt. green, 2 oz. each dk. pink and lt. pink, small amount yellow; tapestry needle; I hook or size needed to obtain gauge.

Gauge: 3 sts = 1"; 3 sc rows = 1"; 3 dc rows = 2".

Skill Level: ★ Easy

Afghan

Row 1: With dk. green, ch 142, dc in 4th ch from hook, dc in each ch across, turn (140 dc).

*Note: Work remaining rows in **back lps** only.*

Rows 2-12: Ch 3, dc in each st across, turn. At end of last row, fasten off.

Row 13: Join med. green with sl st in first st, ch 3, dc in each st across, turn.

Rows 14-24: Ch 3, dc in each st across, turn. At end of last row, fasten off.

Rows 25-36: With lt. green, repeat rows 13-24.

Rows 37-48: With dk. green, repeat rows 13-24.

Rows 49-60: Repeat rows 13-24.

Rows 61-72: With lt. green, repeat rows 13-24.

Rows 73-84: With dk. green, repeat rows 13-24.

Flower Petal
(make 24 dk. pink and 16 lt. pink)

Row 1: Ch 2, 2 sc in 2nd ch from hook, turn (2 sc).

Row 2: Ch 1, 2 sc in each st across, turn (4).

Row 3: Ch 1, 2 sc in first st, sc in each of next 2 sts, 2 sc in last st, turn (6).

Rows 4-7: Ch 1, sc in each st across, turn.

Row 8: Ch 1, sc first 2 sts tog, sc in each of next 2 sts, sc last 2 sts tog, turn (4).

Row 9: Ch 1, sc first 2 sts tog, sc last 2 sts tog, turn (2).

Row 10: Ch 1, sc next 2 sts tog, **do not** turn.

Rnd 11: Working around outer edge, ch 1, sc in end of each row around with 2 sc in each top and bottom sts, join with sl st in first sc, fasten off.

Center
(make 10)

Rnd 1: With yellow, ch 2, 8 sc in 2nd ch from hook, join with sl st in first sc (8 sc).

Rnd 2: Ch 2, (sl st in next st, ch 2) around, join with sl st in joining sl st on last rnd, fasten off.

For **each flower,** working in **back lps** of rnd 11, sew 4 matching petals in a circle on afghan according to Flower Placement Diagram. Sew one Center to center of flower.

Sew flowers to Afghan according to diagram.

Fringe

For **each Fringe,** cut 3 strands each med. green and lt. green each 14" long. Holding all strands together, fold in half, insert hook in st, draw fold through, draw all loose ends through fold, tighten. Trim ends.

Fringe in every 3rd or 4th st across short ends of Afghan. ✍

Flower Placement Diagram

┌Top Edge

Clematis

Designed by Rosetta Harshman

Finished Size: 51" x 69".

Materials: Worsted-weight yarn — 20 oz. royal blue, 17 oz. white, 12 oz. med. blue and 9 oz. green; tapestry needle; G hook or size needed to obtain gauge.

Gauge: Rnds 1-3 of Block = 4¼" across; 4 sts = 1". Each Block is 9" square.

Skill Level: ★★ Average

Block

(make 28)

Rnd 1: With green, ch 10, sl st in first ch to form ring, ch 1, 16 sc in ring, join with sl st in first sc, fasten off (16 sc).

Rnd 2: For **petals,** join royal blue with sl st in any st, (ch 3, tr, ch 3, sl st) in same st, ch 3, skip next st, *(sl st, ch 3, tr, ch 3, sl st) in next st, ch 3, skip next st; repeat from * around, join with sl st in first sl st, fasten off (8 petals, 8 ch-3 sps).

Rnd 3: Join med. blue with sl st in any ch-3 sp between petals, ch 3, (sc, ch 3, sc) in tr at center of next petal, ch 3, *sl st in next ch-3 sp between petals, ch 3, (sc, ch 3, sc) in tr at center of next petal, ch 3; repeat from * around, join, fasten off.

Rnd 4: Working behind petals, join green with sl st in sl st between any 2 petals, (ch 5, sl st in sl st between next 2 petals) around; to **join,** ch 2, dc in first sl st (8 ch sps).

Rnd 5: Ch 1, sc around joining dc, ch 5, (sc in next ch sp, ch 5) around, join with sl st in first sc.

Rnd 6: Sl st in first ch sp, ch 1, (sc, hdc, dc, tr, ch 3, tr, dc, hdc, sc) in same sp, ch 1, *(sc, hdc, dc, tr, ch 3, tr, dc, hdc, sc) in next ch sp, ch 1; repeat from * around, join with sl st in first sc, fasten off.

Rnd 7: Join white with sc in any ch-1 sp, ch 3, sc in same sp, ch 4, (sc, ch 3, sc) in next ch-3 sp, ch 4, *(sc, ch 3, sc) in next ch-1 sp, ch 4, (sc, ch 3, sc) in next ch-3 sp, ch 4; repeat from * around, join, fasten off (16 ch-4 sps, 16 ch-3 sps).

Rnd 8: Join green with sl st in first ch sp, ch 4, 4 tr in same sp, ch 3, sc in next ch-3 sp, ch 3, (5 tr in next ch-3 sp, ch 3, sc in next ch-3 sp, ch 3) around, join with sl st in top of ch-4, fasten off.

Rnd 9: Join white with sl st in 3rd st of any 5-tr group, ch 2, hdc in each st around with 3 hdc in each ch sp, join with sl st in top of ch-2 (96 hdc).

Note: For **double treble crochet (dtr),** yo 3 times, insert hook in next st, yo, draw lp through st, (yo, draw through 2 lps on hook) 4 times.

Rnd 10: For **first corner,** ch 5, (2 dtr, ch 2, 3 dtr) in first st, *[dtr in next st, tr in each of next 2 sts, dc in each of next 2 sts, hdc in next st, sc in next 11 sts, hdc in next st, dc in each of next 2 sts, tr in each of next 2 sts, dtr in next st]; for **corner,** (3 dtr, ch 2, 3 dtr) in next st; repeat from * 2 more times; repeat between [ ], join with sl st in top of ch-5, fasten off (29 sts across each side between corner ch-2 sps).

Rnd 11: Join royal blue with sl st in any corner ch-2 sp, ch 2, (hdc, ch 3, 2 hdc) in same sp, hdc in each st around with (2 hdc, ch 3, 2 hdc) in each corner ch-2 sp, join with sl st in top of ch-2, fasten off (33 hdc across each side between corners).

Sew 7 Blocks together through **back lps** only across one side forming one Panel; repeat making 4 Panels.

Border

Rnd 1: Working around outer edge of one Panel, join royal with sl st in any corner ch sp, ch 3, (dc, ch 2, 2 dc) in same sp, dc in each st, dc in each ch sp on each side of seams and dc in each seam around with (2 dc, ch 2, 2 dc) in each corner ch sp, join with sl st in top of ch-3, fasten off (37 dc across each short end between corner ch sps, 253 dc across each long edge between corner ch sps).

Rnd 2: Join white with sc in any corner ch sp, (sc, ch 2, 2 sc) in same sp, sc in each st

Continued on page 15

Pink Rosebuds

Designed by Tammy Hildebrand

Finished Size: 42" x 64".

Materials: Worsted-weight yarn — 26 oz. fisherman, 7 oz. sage green and 2 oz. pink; I hook or size needed to obtain gauge.

Gauge: 3 dc = 1"; 3 dc rows = 2". Each Strip is 7½" wide.

Skill Level: ★★ Average

Afghan
First Strip

Row 1: With fisherman, ch 9, dc in 4th ch from hook, dc in each ch across, turn (7 dc).

Rows 2-5: Ch 3, dc in each st across, turn. At end of last row, **do not** turn, fasten off.

*Note: For **cluster (cl)**, yo, insert hook in next st, yo, draw lp through, yo, draw through 2 lps on hook, (yo, insert hook in same st, yo, draw lp through, yo, draw through 2 lps on hook) 2 times, yo, draw through all 4 lps on hook.*

Row 6: With right side facing you, join sage green with sl st in first st, ch 4, skip next 2 sts, (cl, ch 1, cl) in next st, ch 2, skip next 2 sts, hdc in last st, **do not** turn, fasten off (2 cls, 2 hdc, 2 ch-2 sps, 1 ch-1 sp).

Row 7: With right side facing you, working over ch-1 sp between cls, join pink with sl st in same st on row before last as cls; for **popcorn (pc),** ch 3, 4 dc in same st, drop lp from hook, insert hook in top of ch-3, draw dropped lp through; **do not** turn, fasten off (1 pc).

Row 8: With right side facing you, join fisherman with sc in 2nd ch of first ch-4 on row before last; working over next ch-2 sp, dc in each of next 2 skipped sts 3 rows below, sc in top of next pc on last row; working over next ch-2, dc in each of next 2 skipped sts 3 rows below, sc in last hdc on row before last, turn (7 sts).

Rows 9-103: Repeat rows 2-8 consecutively, ending with row 5.

Rnd 104: Working around outer edge in sts and in ends of rows, join sage green with sc in first st, ch 2, sc in same st, sc in next 5 sts, (sc, ch 2, sc) in next st, sc in first dc row,
*(ch 1, sc in next dc row) 3 times, 3 dc in next sage row, sc in next dc row; repeat from * across to last 4 dc rows, (ch 1, sc in next row) 4 times; working in starting ch on opposite side of row 1, (sc, ch 2, sc) in first ch, sc in next 5 chs, (sc, ch 2, sc) in next ch, sc in first dc row, (ch 1, sc in next dc row) 4 times, ◊3 dc in next sage row, sc in next dc row, (ch 1, sc in next dc row) 3 times; repeat from ◊ across, join with sl st in first sc, fasten off (7 sc across each short end between corner ch-2 sps, 46 ch-1 sps and 14 3-dc groups across each long edge between corner ch-2 sps).

*Note: For **V-st,** (dc, ch 2, dc) in next st or ch sp.*

Rnd 105: Join fisherman with sl st in first ch-2 sp, ch 3, (dc, ch 2, 2 dc) in same sp, [dc in next st, skip next 2 sts, V-st in ncxt st, skip next 2 sts, dc in next st, (2 dc, ch 2, 2 dc) in next ch-2 sp, dc in next st], V-st in next ch-1 sp, skip next ch-1 sp, V-st in next ch-1 sp, *(sc, ch 2, sc) in center st of next 3-dc group, V-st in next ch-1 sp, skip next ch-1 sp, V-st in next ch-1 sp; repeat from * across to last ch-1 sp before next corner, skip next ch-1 sp, dc in next corner st, (2 dc, ch 2, 2 dc) in next ch-2 sp; repeat between [ ], (skip next ch-1 sp, V-st in next ch-1 sp) 2 times, ◊(sc, ch 2, sc) in center st of next 3-dc group, V-st in next ch-1 sp, skip next ch-1 sp, V-st in next ch-1 sp; repeat from ◊ across to last 2 sts before next ch-2 sp, skip next st, dc in last st, join with sl st in top of ch-3.

Rnd 106: Sl st in next st, sl st in next ch-2 sp, ch 3, (2 dc, ch 2, 3 dc) in same sp, [skip next 3 dc, V-st in sp between last skipped dc and next V-st, V-st in sp between last dc of same V-st and next dc, (3 dc, ch 2, 3 dc) in next corner ch-2 sp, skip next 3 dc, V-st in sp between last skipped dc and next V-st, V-st in sp between next 2 V-sts, *V-st in sp between next V-st and next sc, V-st in sp between next sc and next V-st, V-st in sp between next 2 V-sts; repeat from * across to last V-st before next corner ch-2 sp, V-st in sp between last dc

Continued on page 14

Pink Rosebuds

Continued from page 12

of last V-st and next dc], (3 dc, ch 2, 3 dc) in next corner ch-2 sp; repeat between [ ], join

Rnd 107: Sl st in each of next 2 sts, sl st in next ch-2 sp, ch 2, (hdc, ch 2, 2 hdc) in same sp, [skip next st, 2 hdc in next st, skip next st, hdc in sp between last skipped st and next V-st, 2 hdc in ch sp of next V-st, hdc in sp between last V-st and next V-st, 2 hdc in ch sp of next V-st, hdc in sp between last V-st and next st, skip next st, 2 hdc in next st, (2 hdc, ch 2, 2 hdc) in next corner ch-2 sp, skip next st, 2 hdc in next st, skip next st, hdc in sp between last skipped st and next V-st, 2 hdc in ch sp of next V-st, (hdc in sp between last V-st and next V-st, 2 hdc in ch sp of next V-st) across to last 3 dc before next corner ch-2 sp, hdc in sp between last V-st and next st, skip next st, 2 hdc in next st, skip next st], (2 hdc, ch 2, 2 hdc) in next corner ch-2 sp; repeat between [ ], join with sl st in top of ch-2.

Rnd 108: Ch 3, dc in each st around with (3 dc, ch 2, 3 dc) in each corner ch-2 sp, join with sl st in top of ch-3, fasten off (21 dc across each short end between corner ch sps, 150 dc across each long edge between corner ch sps).

Rnd 109: Join sage green with sc in 2nd corner ch-2 sp, ch 5, sc in same sp, ◊*skip next 2 sts, (sc, ch 3, sc) in next st*; repeat between **, [skip next st, (sc, ch 3, sc) in next st]; repeat between [ ] across to 2 sts before next corner ch-2 sp, skip next 2 sts, (sc, ch 5, sc) in next corner ch-2 sp; repeat between ** 3 times; repeat between [ ] 2 times; repeat between ** 2 times, skip next 2 sts◊, (sc, ch 5, sc) in next corner ch-2 sp; repeat between ◊◊, join with sl st in first sc, fasten off (7 ch-3 sps across each short end between corner ch-5 sps, 73 ch-3 sps across each long side between corner ch-5 sps).

Next Strip

Rows/Rnds 1-108: Repeat same rows/rnds of First Strip on page 12.

*Notes: For **joining ch-5 sp,** ch 2, drop lp from hook, insert hook in center ch of corresponding ch-5 sp on previous Strip, draw dropped lp through, ch 2.*

*For **joining ch-3 sp,** ch 1, drop lp from hook, insert hook in center ch of corresponding ch-3 sp on previous Strip, draw dropped lp through, ch 1.*

Rnd 109: Join sage green with sc in 2nd corner ch sp, joining ch-5 sp, sc in same sp as last sc on this Strip, (skip next 2 sts, sc in next st, joining ch-3 sp, sc in same st as last sc on this Strip) 2 times, (skip next st, sc in next st, joining ch-3 sp, sc in same st as last sc on this Strip) across to 2 sts before next corner ch-2 sp, skip next 2 sts, sc in next corner ch sp, joining ch-5 sp, sc in same sp as last sc on this Strip, ◊*skip next 2 sts, (sc, ch 3, sc) in next st*; repeat between ** 2 more times, [skip next st, (sc, ch 3, sc) in next st]; repeat between [ ]; repeat between ** 2 times◊, (sc, ch 5, sc) in next ch sp; repeat between ** 2 times; repeat between [ ] across to 2 sts before next corner ch sp, skip next 2 sts, (sc, ch 5, sc) in next ch sp; repeat between ◊◊, join with sl st in first sc, fasten off.

Repeat Next Strip 3 more times for a total of 5 Strips.

Border

Rnd 1: Working over corner ch-5 of last rnd into corner ch sp of rnd before last, join fisherman with sl st in corner ch sp before one short end, ch 3, (dc, ch 2, 2 dc) in same sp, [V-st in next ch-3 sp on last rnd, (dc in next ch-3 sp, V-st in next ch-3 sp) 3 times, *(tr, ch 2, tr) in side of next joining, V-st in next ch-3 sp, (dc in next ch-3 sp, V-st in next ch-3 sp) 3 times; repeat from * across to next corner ch-5 sp; working over corner ch sp of last rnd into corner ch sp of rnd before last, (2 dc, ch 2, 2 dc) in next ch sp, V-st in next ch-3 sp on last rnd, (dc in next ch-3 sp, V-st in next ch-3 sp) across to next corner ch-5 sp]; working over corner ch sp of last rnd into corner ch sp of rnd before last, (2 dc, ch 2, 2 dc) in next ch sp; repeat between [ ], join with sl st in top of ch-3 .

Rnd 2: Sl st in next st, sl st in next ch-2 sp, ch 2, (hdc, ch 2, 2 hdc) in same sp, ◊skip next 2 sts, hdc in sp between last skipped st and next V-st, *[2 hdc in next V-st, (hdc in sp between same V-st and next dc, hdc in sp between same dc and next V-st, 2 hdc in next V-st) 3 times], hdc in sp between same V-st and next tr, 2 hdc in next ch-2 sp, hdc in sp between next tr and next dc; repeat from * 3 more times; repeat between [ ], hdc in sp between same V-st and next dc, (2 hdc, ch 2, 2 hdc) in next corner ch-2 sp, skip next 2 sts, hdc in sp between last skipped st and next V-st, 2 hdc in next V-st, hdc in sp between same V-st and next dc, (hdc in sp between same dc and next V-st, 2 hdc in next V-st, hdc in sp between same V-st and next dc) across to next corner ch-2 sp◊, (2 hdc, ch 2, 2 hdc) in next ch-2 sp; repeat between ◊◊, join with sl st in top of ch-2.

Rnd 3: Ch 3, dc in each st around with (2 dc, ch 2, 2 dc) in each corner ch-2 sp, join with

sl st in top of ch-3, fasten off (96 dc across each short end, 156 dc across each long side).

Rnd 4: Join sage green with sl st in corner ch sp before one short end, ch 3, 4 dc in same sp, [sl st in next st, skip next st, 5 dc in next st, (skip next st, sl st in next st, skip next st, 5 dc in next st) 11 times, sl st in each of next 2 sts, 5 dc in next st, (skip next st, sl st in next st, skip next st, 5 dc in next st) 11 times, skip next st, sl st in next st, 5 dc in next corner ch-2 sp, sl st in next st, skip next 2 sts, 7 dc in next st, (skip next 2 sts, sl st in next st, skip next 2 sts, 7 dc in next st) 12 times, skip next st, sl st in each of next 2 sts, skip next st, 7 dc in next st, (skip next 2 sts, sl st in next st, skip next 2 sts, 7 dc in next st) 12 times, skip next 2 sts, sl st in next st], 5 dc in next corner ch-2 sp; repeat between [ ], join, fasten off. ✍

Clematis

Continued from page 11

around with (2 sc, ch 2, 2 sc) in each corner ch sp, join with sl st in first sc, fasten off (41 dc across each short end between corner ch sps, 257 dc across each long edge between corner ch sps).

Rnd 3: Join med. blue with sl st in any corner ch sp, ch 3, (dc, ch 3, 2 dc) in same sp, dc in each st around with (2 dc, ch 3, 2 dc) in each corner ch sp, join with sl st in top of ch-3, fasten off (45 dc across each short end between corner ch sps, 261 dc across each long edge between corner ch sps).

Holding Panels wrong sides together, matching sts, with med. green, sew long edges between corner ch sps together through **back lps.**

Edging

Rnd 1: Working around entire outer edge, join med. blue with sl st in corner ch sp before one short end, ch 3, (dc, ch 2, 2 dc) in same sp, dc in each st, dc in each ch sp on each side of seams and dc in each seam around with (2 dc,

ch 2, 2 dc) in each corner ch sp, join with sl st in top of ch-3, fasten off (193 dc across each short end between corner ch sps, 265 dc across each long edge between corner ch sps).

Note: *For **horizontal cluster (h-cl),** ch 4, yo, insert hook in 4th ch from hook, yo, draw lp through, yo, draw through 2 lps on hook, yo, insert hook in same ch, yo, draw lp through, yo, draw through 2 lps on hook, yo, draw through all 3 lps on hook.*

Rnd 2: Join royal blue with sc in first corner ch-2 sp, (h-cl, sc) 2 times in same sp, *[(h-cl, skip next 2 sts, sc in next st) 2 times, h-cl, skip next 3 sts, (sc in next st, h-cl, skip next 3 sts) across to next corner ch sp], (sc, h-cl, sc, h-cl, sc) in next ch sp; repeat from * 2 more times; repeat between [ ], join with sl st in first sc, fasten off.

Rnd 3: Join med. blue with sc in any sc, ch 2, (sc, ch 3, sc) in ch-3 sp of next h-cl, ch 2, *sc in next sc, ch 2, (sc, ch 3, sc) in ch-3 sp of next h-cl, ch 2; repeat from * around, join, fasten off. ✍

Lush Delights

Designed by Martha Brooks Stein

Finished Size: 50" x 64".

Materials: Fuzzy worsted-weight yarn — 24 oz. off-white, 16 oz. spruce, 3 oz. each lt. peach, dk. peach, red, lt. rose, dk. rose and yellow for flower colors, 2 oz. gold; I hook or size needed to obtain gauge.

Gauge: Rnds 1-2 of Block = 4" across. Each Block is 7" square.

Skill Level: ★★ Average

First Row
First Block

Rnd 1: With gold, ch 4, sl st in first ch to form ring, ch 1, 8 sc in ring, join with sl st in first sc, fasten off (8 sc).

Note: *When working rnd 2, use flower color in order shown on Assembly Diagram (see page 25).*

Rnd 2: Join flower color (see Assembly Diagram) with sl st in any st, ch 3, 5 dc in same st, **turn,** ch 3, dc in next 5 dc just made, **turn,** ch 4, (6 dc in next st on last rnd, **turn,** ch 3, dc in next 5 dc just made, **turn,** ch 4) around, join with sl st in top of first ch-3 (8 petals, 8 ch sps).

Rnd 3: Join green with sc in any ch-4 sp, ch 2, (2 dc, ch 3, 3 dc) in next ch-4 sp, ch 2, *sc in next ch-4 sp, ch 2, (3 dc, ch 3, 3 dc) in next ch-4 sp, ch 2; repeat from * around, join with sl st in first sc, fasten off (8 ch-2 sps, 4 ch-3 sps).

Rnd 4: Join off-white with sl st in any corner ch-3 sp, ch 3, (2 dc, ch 2, 3 dc) in same sp, ch 1, (3 dc in next ch-2 sp, ch 1) 2 times, *(3 dc, ch 2, 3 dc) in next ch-3 sp, ch 1, (3 dc in next ch-2 sp, ch 1) 2 times; repeat from * around, join with sl st in top of ch-3 (12 ch-1 sps, 4 ch-2 sps).

Rnd 5: Sl st in each of next 2 sts, sl st in next ch sp, ch 3, (2 dc, ch 2, 3 dc) in same sp, ch 1, (3 dc in next ch-1 sp, ch 1) 3 times, *(3 dc, ch 2, 3 dc) in next ch-2 sp, ch 1, (3 dc in next ch-1 sp, ch 1) 3 times; repeat from * around, join, fasten off (16 ch-1 sps, 4 ch-2 sps).

Second Block

Rnds 1-4: Repeat same rnds of First Block.

Rnd 5: Sl st in each of next 2 sts, sl st in next ch sp, ch 3, (2 dc, ch 2, 3 dc) in same sp, ch 1, (3 dc in next ch-1 sp, ch 1) 3 times, (3 dc, ch 2, 3 dc) in next ch-2 sp, ch 1, (3 dc in next ch-1 sp, ch 1) 3 times, 3 dc in next ch-2 sp, ch 1; joining to side of last Block made (see Joining Diagram on page 25), sc in corresponding ch-2 sp on other Block, 3 dc in same ch-2 sp on this Block, sc in next ch-1 sp on other Block, (3 dc in next ch-1 sp on this Block, sc in next ch-1 sp on other Block) 3 times, 3 dc in next ch-2 sp on this Block, sc in next ch-2 sp on other Block, ch 1, 3 dc in same ch-2 sp on this Block, ch 1, (3 dc in next ch-1 sp, ch 1) 3 times, join, fasten off.

Repeat Second Block 4 more times for a total of 6 Blocks.

Second Row
First Block

Joining to bottom of First Block on last row, work same as First Row Second Block.

Second Block

Rnds 1-4: Repeat same rnds of First Row First Block.

Rnd 5: Sl st in each of next 2 sts, sl st in next ch sp, ch 3, (2 dc, ch 2, 3 dc) in same sp, ch 1, (3 dc in next ch-1 sp, ch 1) 3 times, 3 dc in next ch-2 sp, ch 1; joining to bottom of Next Block on last row, sc in corresponding ch-2 sp on other Block, *3 dc in same ch-2 sp on this Block, sc in next ch-1 sp on other Block, (3 dc in next ch-1 sp on this Block, sc in next ch-1 sp on other Block) 3 times, 3 dc in next ch-2 sp on this Block, sc in next ch-2 sp on other Block*; joining to side of last Block on this row, sc in next ch-2 sp on other Block; repeat between **, ch 1, 3 dc in same ch-2 sp on this Block, ch 1, (3 dc in next ch-1 sp, ch 1) 3 times, join, fasten off.

Repeat Second Block 4 more times for a total of 6 Blocks.

Repeat Second Row 6 more times for a total of 8 Rows.

Continued on page 25

Floral Tiles

Designed by Jennifer Christiansen McClain

Finished Size: 29" x 33".

Materials: Baby sport yarn — 11 oz. green, 5½ oz. each yellow and pink; I hook or size needed to obtain gauge.

Gauge: Rnds 1-4 of Large Motif = 1¾" across. Each Large Motif is 4½" across.

Skill Level: ★★ Average

Large Motif
(make 42)

Rnd 1: With yellow, ch 4, sl st in first ch to form ring, ch 1, 8 sc in ring, join with sl st in first sc (8 sc).

Rnd 2: Working this rnd in **front lps** only, ch 3, (sl st in next st, ch 3) around, join with sl st in joining sl st of last rnd.

Rnd 3: Working in **back lps** of rnd 1, ch 1, 2 sc in each st around, join with sl st in first sc (16 sc).

Rnd 4: Ch 1, sc in first st, ch 1, skip next st, (sc in next st, ch 1, skip next st) around, join, fasten off (8 sc, 8 ch sps).

Rnd 5: Working over ch sps on last rnd, join green with sc in any skipped st on rnd before last, ch 2, sc in same st, ch 1, skip next st on last rnd, *(sc, ch 2, sc) in next skipped st on rnd before last, ch 1, skip next st on last rnd; repeat from * around, join, fasten off (8 ch-2 sps, 8 ch-1 sps).

Rnd 6: Sl st in next ch-2 sp, ch 1, (sc, ch 2, sc) in same sp, ch 1, skip next ch-1 sp, *(sc, ch 2, sc) in next ch-2 sp, ch 1, skip next ch-1 sp; repeat from * around, join, fasten off.

Rnd 7: Join pink with sc in any ch-2 sp, ch 2, sc in same sp; working behind next ch-1 sp, 3 dc in next ch-1 sp on rnd before last, *(sc, ch 2, sc) in next ch-2 sp on last rnd; working behind next ch-1 sp, 3 dc in next ch-1 sp on rnd before last; repeat from * around, join (24 dc, 8 ch-2 sps).

Rnd 8: Sl st in next ch-2 sp, ch 1, (sc, ch 2, sc) in same sp, skip next sc, sc in each of next 3 dc, *(sc, ch 2, sc) in next ch-2 sp, skip next sc, sc in each of next 3 dc; repeat from *

around, join, fasten off (40 sc, 8 ch-2 sps).

Rnd 9: Working behind ch-2 sps on last rnd, join yellow with sc in any ch-2 sp between sc on rnd before last, ch 2, sc in same sp, *[ch 1, skip next st on last rnd, (sc in next st, ch 1, skip next st) 2 times], (sc, ch 2, sc) in next ch-2 sp between sc on rnd before last; repeat from * 6 more times; repeat between [ ], join, fasten off (24 ch-1 sps, 8 ch-2 sps).

Rnd 10: Working over ch-2 sps on last rnd, join green with sc in any ch-2 sp on rnd before last, ch 2, sc in same sp, *[sc in next ch-1 sp on last rnd; working over next ch-1 sp, 3 sc in next skipped sc on rnd before last, sc in next ch-1 sp on last rnd], (sc, ch 2, sc) in next ch-2 sp on rnd before last; repeat from * 6 more times; repeat between [ ], join, fasten off (7 sc across each side between ch sps).

Filler Motif
(make 30)

Rnds 1-4: Repeat same rnds of Large Motif.

Rnd 5: Working over ch sps on last rnd in skipped sts on rnd before last, join green with sc in any st, 2 sc in same st, (hdc, dc, ch 2, dc, hdc) in next st, *3 sc in next st, (hdc, dc, ch 2, dc, hdc) in next st; repeat from * around, join, fasten off (7 sts across each side between ch sps).

Holding Motifs right sides together, matching sts, with green, sc Large Motifs and Filler Motifs together through **front lps** according to Assembly Diagram (see page 25).

Edging

Rnd 1: Working around outer edge, in **back lps** only, join yellow with sl st in any st, ch 2, skip next st, (sl st in next st, ch or seam, ch 2, skip next st, ch or seam) around, join with sl st in first sl st, fasten off.

Rnd 2: Working over ch sps of last rnd,
Continued on page 25

Roses in Lace

Designed by Maggie Weldon

Finished Size: 39" x 54".

Materials: Worsted-weight yarn — 20 oz. dk. peach, 18 oz. beige and 11 oz. green; I hook or size needed to obtain gauge.

Gauge: Rnds 1-4 of Block = 3¼" across. Each Block is 5" square.

Skill Level: ★★ Average

First Row
First Block

Rnd 1: With dk. peach, ch 4, sl st in first ch to form ring, ch 1, (sc in ring, ch 2) 8 times, join with sl st in first sc (8 sc, 8 ch sps).

Rnd 2: For **petals,** (sc, 3 dc, sl st) in each ch sp around, join (8 petals).

Rnd 3: Working behind last rnd, ch 2, sl st in last sl st of first petal, (ch 2, sl st in last sl st of next petal) around, **do not** join.

Rnd 4: (Sc, 5 dc, sl st) in each ch sp around, join with sl st in first sc, fasten off.

Rnd 5: Join green with sl st in 3rd dc of any petal on last rnd, ch 4, (2 tr, ch 3, 3 tr) in same st, (dc, ch 5, dc) in 3rd dc of next petal, *(3 tr, ch 3, 3 tr) in 3rd dc of next petal, (dc, ch 5, dc) in 3rd dc of next petal; repeat from * around, join with sl st in top of ch-4, fasten off (32 sts, 4 ch-5 sps, 4 ch-3 sps).

Rnd 6: Join beige with sc in any ch-5 sp, *[ch 4, skip next 2 sts, dc in each of next 2 sts, (3 tr, ch 3, 3 tr) in next ch-3 sp, dc in each of next 2 sts, ch 4, skip next 2 sts], sc in next ch-5 sp; repeat from * 2 more times; repeat between [ ], join with sl st in first sc, fasten off (8 ch-4, 4 ch-3 sps).

Second Block

Rnds 1-5: Repeat same rnds of First Block.

Rnd 6: Join beige with sc in any ch-5 sp, ch 4, skip next 2 sts, dc in each of next 2 sts, *(3 tr, ch 3, 3 tr) in next ch-3 sp, dc in each of next 2 sts, ch 4, skip next 2 sts, sc in next ch-5 sp, ch 4, skip next 2 sts, dc in each of next 2 sts; repeat from *, 3 tr in next ch-3 sp; joining to side of last Block made (see Joining Diagram on page 24), ch 1, drop lp from hook, insert hook in corresponding ch-3 sp on other Block, draw dropped lp through, ch 1, 3 tr in same ch-3 sp on this Block, dc in each of next 2 sts, [ch 2, drop lp from hook, insert hook in next ch-4 sp on other Block, draw dropped lp through, ch 2, skip next 2 sts on this Block], sc in next ch-5 sp; repeat between [ ], dc in each of next 2 sts, 3 tr in next ch-3 sp, ch 1, drop lp from hook, insert hook in corresponding ch-3 sp on other Block, draw dropped lp through, ch 1, 3 tr in same ch-3 sp on this Block, dc in each of next 2 sts, ch 4, skip last 2 sts, join with sl st in first sc, fasten off.

Repeat Second Block 5 more times for a total of 7 Blocks.

Second Row
First Block

Joining to bottom of First Block on last row, work same as First Row Second Block.

Second Block

Rnds 1-5: Repeat same rnds of First Row First Block.

Rnd 6: Join beige with sc in any ch-5 sp, ch 4, skip next 2 sts, dc in each of next 2 sts, (3 tr, ch 3, 3 tr) in next ch-3 sp, dc in each of next 2 sts, ch 4, skip next 2 sts, sc in next ch-5 sp, ch 4, skip next 2 sts, dc in each of next 2 sts; joining to bottom of Next Block on last row, 3 tr in next ch-3 sp, ch 1, drop lp from hook, insert hook in corresponding ch-3 sp on other Block, draw dropped lp through, ch 1, 3 tr in same ch-3 sp on this Block, *dc in each of next 2 sts, [ch 2, drop lp from hook, insert hook in next ch-4 sp on other Block, draw dropped lp through, ch 2, skip next 2 sts on this Block], sc in next ch-5 sp; repeat between [ ], dc in each of next 2 sts, 3 tr in next ch-3 sp, ch 1, drop lp from hook, insert hook in corresponding ch-3 sp on other

Continued on page 24

Painted Daisy

Designed by Maggie Weldon

Finished Size: 53" x 68".

Materials: Worsted-weight yarn — 35 oz. white, 11 oz. rose and 2 oz. yellow; I hook or size needed to obtain gauge.

Gauge: Rnd 1 of Large Motif = 3⅜" across. Each Large Motif is 7½" across.

Skill Level: ★★ Average

First Row
First Large Motif

Notes: For **beginning cluster (beg cl),** ch 4, *yo 2 times, insert hook in same sp, yo, draw lp through, (yo, draw through 2 lps on hook) 2 times; repeat from *, yo, draw through all 3 lps on hook.

For **cluster (cl),** *yo 2 times, insert hook in next sp, yo, draw lp through, (yo, draw through 2 lps on hook) 2 times; repeat from * 2 more times in same sp, yo, draw through all 4 lps on hook.

For **picot,** ch 4, sl st in top of last st made.

Rnd 1: With rose, ch 4, sl st in first ch to form ring, beg cl, picot, ch 3, (cl in ring, picot, ch 3) 7 times, join with sl st in top of beg cl, fasten off (8 cls, 8 picots, 8 ch-3 sps).

Rnd 2: Join white with sl st in any picot, ch 3, 2 dc in same sp, 7 dc in each picot around, 4 dc in same sp as first st, join with sl st in top of ch-3 (56 dc).

Rnd 3: Ch 1, sc in first st, ch 4, skip next st, sc next 2 sts tog, ch 4, skip next st, *(sc in next st, ch 4, skip next st) 2 times, sc next 2 sts tog, ch 4, skip next st; repeat from * around to last 2 sts, sc in next st, ch 4, skip last st, join with sl st in first sc (24 ch sps).

Rnd 4: Sl st in first ch sp, ch 1, sc in same sp, ch 7, sc in next ch sp, dc in next ch sp, (picot, dc) 3 times in same sp, *sc in next ch sp, ch 7, sc in next ch sp, dc in next ch sp, (picot, dc) 3 times in same sp; repeat from * around, join, fasten off (24 picots, 8 ch-7 sps).

Second Large Motif

Rnds 1-3: Repeat same rnds of First Large Motif.

Notes: For **joining picot,** ch 2, drop lp from hook, insert hook in corresponding picot on other Motif (see Joining Diagram on page 24), draw dropped lp through, ch 2.

For **joining ch-7 sp,** ch 3, drop lp from hook, insert hook in center ch of next ch-7 sp on other Motif, draw dropped lp through, ch 3.

Rnd 4: Sl st in first ch sp, ch 1, sc in same sp, ch 7, sc in next ch sp, *dc in next ch sp, (picot, dc) 3 times in same sp, sc in next ch sp, ch 7, sc in next ch sp; repeat from * 5 more times, dc in next ch sp, picot, dc in same ch sp; joining to side of last Motif (see diagram), (joining picot, dc in same ch sp on this Motif) 2 times, sc in next ch sp, joining ch-7 sp, sc in next ch sp on this Motif, dc in next ch sp, (joining picot, dc in same ch sp on this Motif) 2 times, picot, dc in same ch sp, join, fasten off.

Repeat Second Motif 5 more times for a total of 7 Motifs.

Second Row
First Large Motif

Joining to bottom of First Large Motif on last row, work same as First Row Second Large Motif.

Second Large Motif

Rnds 1-3: Repeat same rnds of First Row First Large Motif.

Rnd 4: Sl st in first ch sp, ch 1, sc in same sp, ch 7, sc in next ch sp, *dc in next ch sp, (picot, dc) 3 times in same sp, sc in next ch sp, ch 7, sc in next ch sp; repeat from * 3 more times, dc in next ch sp, picot, dc in same ch sp; joining to side of next Motif on last row, ◊(joining picot, dc in same ch sp on this Motif) 2 times, sc in next ch sp, joining ch-7 sp, sc in next ch sp on this Motif, dc in next ch sp, (joining picot, dc in same ch sp on this Motif) 2 times , picot, dc in same ch sp◊, sc in next ch sp, ch 7, sc in next ch sp, dc in next ch sp, picot, dc in same ch sp; joining to

Continued on page 24

Painted Daisy

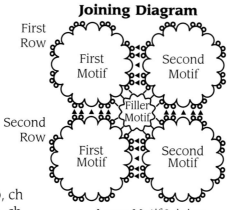

Continued from page 22

side of last Motif on this row; repeat between ◊◊, join, fasten off.

Repeat Second Motif 5 more times for a total of 7 Motifs.

Repeat Second Row 7 more times for a total of 9 rows.

Filler Motif
(make 48)

Rnd 1: With white, ch 2, 6 sc in 2nd ch from hook, join with sl st in first sc (6 sc).

Rnd 2: Ch 1, sc in first st, ch 3, (sc in next st, ch 3) around, join (6 ch sps).

Rnd 3: Sl st in first ch sp, ch 1, (sc, ch 3, sc) in same sp, ch 3, *(sc, ch 3, sc) in next ch sp,

ch 3; repeat from * around, join (12 ch sps).

Notes: *For **joining ch-5 sp,** ch 2, drop lp from hook, insert hook in corresponding picot or in center ch of corresponding ch-7 sp on other Motif, ch 2.*

Join Filler Motifs to sps between Large Motifs according to Joining Diagram.

Rnd 4: Sl st in first ch sp, ch 1, sc in same sp, joining ch-5 sp, (sc in next ch sp on Filler Motif, joining ch-5 sp) around, join, fasten off.

Flower Center
(make 63)

With yellow, ch 2, 6 sc in 2nd ch from hook, join with sl st in first sc, fasten off.

Sew one Flower Center to center of each Large Motif. ✑

Joining Diagram

◄ = Large Motif Joining
↘ = Filler Motif Joining

Roses in Lace

Continued from page 21

Block, draw dropped lp through, ch 1, 3 tr in same ch-3 sp on this Block*; joining to side of last Block on this row, repeat between **, dc in each of next 2 sts, ch 4, skip last 2 sts, join with sl st in first sc, fasten off.

Repeat Second Block 5 more times for a total of 7 Blocks.

Repeat Second Row 8 more times for a total of 10 rows.

Border

Note: *For **V-st,** (dc, ch 2, dc) in next st or ch sp.*

Rnd 1: Working around outer edge, join beige with sl st in any corner ch-3 sp, ch 5, (dc, ch 2, dc, ch 2, dc) in same sp, ◊•*[ch 2, skip next 2 sts, V-st in next st, ch 2, (V-st in next ch-4 sp, ch 2) 2 times, skip next 2 sts, V-st in next st, ch 2], (V-st in next joined ch sp, ch 2) 2 times; repeat from * across to last Block before next corner; repeat between [ ]•,

dc in next corner ch-3 sp, (ch 2, dc) 3 times in same sp; repeat from ◊ 2 more times; repeat between ••, join with sl st in 3rd ch of ch-5, fasten off.

Rnd 2: Join dk. peach with sl st in last ch-2 sp made on last rnd, dc in next ch-2 sp, (ch 1, dc) 4 times in same sp, *sl st in next ch-2 sp, dc in next ch-2 sp, (ch 1, dc) 4 times in same sp; repeat from * around, join with sl st in first sl st, fasten off.

Rnd 3: Join beige with sl st in first sl st, sc in next ch-1 sp, (ch 4, sc in next ch-1 sp) 3 times, *sl st in next sl st, sc in next ch-1 sp, (ch 4, sc in next ch-1 sp) 3 times; repeat from * around, join, fasten off. ✑

Joining Diagram

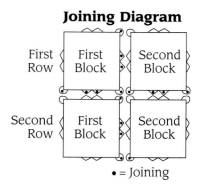

• = Joining

Floral Tiles

Continued from page 18

join pink with sl st in any skipped st on Motif, (ch 2, drop lp from hook, insert hook in next skipped st, ch or seam on Motif, pick up dropped lp from behind yellow lp, draw lp through) around, ch 2, drop lp from hook, insert hook in same st as joining sl st, pick up dropped lp, draw through st, fasten off. ✎

Assembly Diagram

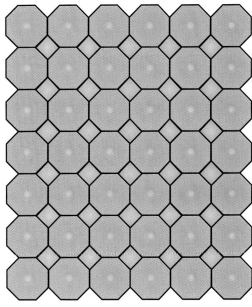

Lush Delights

Continued from page 17

Border

Rnd 1: Working around outer edge, join off-white with sc in any corner ch-2 sp, sc in same sp, sc in each st, sc in each ch-1 sp, sc in each ch sp on each side of joining and sc in each joining sc around with 2 sc in each corner ch-2 sp, join with sl st in first sc, fasten off (131 sc across each short end, 175 sc across each long edge).

Rnd 2: Join green with sl st in 2nd sc, ch 3, dc in each of next 2 sts, (ch 1, skip next st, dc in each of next 3 sts) across to next corner, ch 4, *dc in each of next 3 sts, (ch 1, skip next st, dc in each of next 3 sts) across to next corner, ch 4; repeat from * around, join with sl st in top of ch-3, fasten off.

Rnd 3: Join off-white with sl st in any corner ch sp, ch 3, (2 dc, ch 2, 3 dc) in same sp, *[ch 1, skip next 2 sts, dc in next st, dc in next ch-1 sp, dc in next st, (ch 1, skip next st, dc in next st, dc in next ch-1 sp, dc in next st) around to last 2 sts before next corner ch sp, ch 1, skip next 2

sts], (3 dc, ch 2, 3 dc) in next ch sp; repeat from * 2 more times; repeat between [ ], join, fasten off.

Rnd 4: With green, repeat rnd 3.

Rnd 5: Repeat rnd 3.

Rnd 6: With green, repeat rnd 3, **do not** fasten off.

Rnd 7: Ch 1, sc in each st and in each ch-1 sp around with 2 sc in each corner ch sp, join with sl st in first sc, fasten off. ✎

Assembly Diagram

Joining Diagram

	First Block	Second Block
First Row	First Block	Second Block
Second Row	First Block	Second Block

❋ = Dk. Pink   ❋ = Red
❋ = Dk. Peach   ❋ = Yellow
❋ = Lt. Pink   ❋ = Lt. Peach

Forget-Me-Not

Designed by Maggie Weldon

Finished Size: 45" x 58".

Materials: Fuzzy worsted-weight yarn — 28 oz. mint, 14 oz. blue and 3½ oz. yellow; K hook or size needed to obtain gauge.

Gauge: Rnds 1-3 of Hexagon = 4½" across. Each Hexagon is 6¾" across.

Skill Level: ★★ Average

First Row
First Hexagon

Rnd 1: With yellow, ch 6, sl st in first ch to form ring, ch 1, 12 sc in ring, join with sl st in first sc, fasten off (12 sc).

Rnd 2: Join blue with sl st in any st, ch 5, (dc in next st, ch 2) around, join with sl st in 3rd ch of ch-5 (12 dc, 12 ch sps).

Rnd 3: Ch 1, sc in first st, 6 dc in next st, (sc in next st, 6 dc in next st) around, join with sl st in first sc, fasten off (36 dc, 6 sc).

Rnd 4: Join mint with sc in any sc, ch 5, sc in sp between 3rd and 4th sts of next 6-dc group, ch 5, (sc in next sc, ch 5, sc in sp between 3rd and 4th sts of next 6-dc group, ch 5) around, join (12 ch sps).

Rnd 5: Sl st in first ch sp, ch 3, (2 dc, ch 2, 3 dc) in same sp, 2 dc in next ch sp, *(3 dc, ch 2, 3 dc) in next ch sp, 2 dc in next ch sp; repeat from * around, join with sl st in top of ch-3 (48 dc, 6 ch sps).

Rnd 6: Ch 1, sc in first st, ch 5, skip next 2 sts, (sc, ch 5, sc) in next ch sp, ch 5, skip next 2 sts, *(sc in next st, ch 5, skip next 2 sts) 2 times, (sc, ch 5, sc) in next ch sp, ch 5, skip next 2 sts; repeat from * 4 more times, sc in next st, ch 5, skip last 2 sts, join with sl st in first sc, fasten off (24 ch sps).

Next Hexagon

Rnds 1-5: Repeat same rnds of First Hexagon.

Notes: For **joining ch-5 sp**, *ch 2, sl st in corresponding ch sp on other Hexagon (see Joining Diagram on page 31), ch 2.*

This Hexagon is joined across one side.

Rnd 6: Ch 1, sc in first st, ch 5, skip next 2 sts, *(sc, ch 5, sc) in next ch sp, ch 5, skip next 2 sts, (sc in next st, ch 5, skip next 2 sts) 2 times; repeat from * 3 more times; joining to side of last Hexagon, (sc, joining ch-5 sp, sc) in next ch sp on this Hexagon, joining ch-5 sp, skip next 2 sts on this Hexagon, (sc in next st, joining ch-5 sp, skip next 2 sts on this Hexagon) 2 times, (sc, joining ch-5 sp, sc) in next ch sp on this Hexagon, ch 5, skip next 2 sts, sc in next st, ch 5, skip last 2 sts, join with sl st in first sc, fasten off.

Repeat Next Hexagon 6 more times for a total of 8 Hexagons.

Second Row
First Hexagon

Rnds 1-5: Repeat same rnds of First Row First Hexagon.

Note: *This Hexagon is joined across 2 sides.*

Rnd 6: Ch 1, sc in first st, ch 5, skip next 2 sts, *(sc, ch 5, sc) in next ch sp, ch 5, skip next 2 sts, (sc in next st, ch 5, skip next 2 sts) 2 times; repeat from * 2 more times; joining to bottom of second Hexagon on last row (see diagram), (sc, joining ch-5 sp, sc) in next ch sp on this Hexagon, joining ch-5 sp, skip next 2 sts on this Hexagon, (sc in next st, joining ch-5 sp, skip next 2 sts on this Hexagon) 2 times, sc in next ch sp, joining ch-5 sp in side of next joining ch-5 sp on last row, sc in same ch sp on this Hexagon; joining to bottom of First Hexagon on last row, joining ch-5 sp, skip next 2 sts on this Hexagon, (sc in next st, joining ch-5 sp, skip next 2 sts on this Hexagon) 2 times, (sc, joining ch-5 sp, sc) in next ch sp, ch 5, skip next 2 sts, sc in next st, ch 5, skip last 2 sts, join with sl st in first sc, fasten off.

Next Hexagon

Rnds 1-5: Repeat same rnds of First Row First Hexagon.

Continued on page 31

Rose Trellis

Designed by Maggie Weldon

Finished Size: 51" x 74".

Materials: Worsted-weight yarn — 28 oz. aran, 21 oz. burgundy and 7 oz. green; I hook or size needed to obtain gauge.

Gauge: Rnds 1-8 of Hexagon = 5" across. Each Hexagon is 8" across.

Skill Level: ★★★ Advanced

First Row
First Hexagon

Rnd 1: With burgundy, ch 3, sl st in first ch to form ring, ch 1, (sc in ring, ch 2) 6 times, join with sl st in first sc (6 ch sps).

Rnd 2: (Sc, 3 dc, sc, sl st) in each ch sp around, join (6 petals).

Rnd 3: Working behind petals, ch 3, sl st in last sl st of first Motif, (ch 3, sl st in last sl st of next petal) around, **do not** join.

Rnd 4: (Sc, 5 dc, sc, sl st) in each ch sp around, join with sl st in first sc.

Rnd 5: Working behind petals, ch 4, sl st in last sl st on first petal, (ch 3, sl st in last sl st on next petal) around, **do not** join.

Rnd 6: (Sc, 7 dc, sc, sl st) in each ch sp around, join with sl st in first sc.

Rnd 7: Working behind petals, ch 5, sl st in last sl st on first petal, (ch 3, sl st in last sl st on next petal) around, **do not** join, fasten off.

*Note: For **cluster (cl)**, *yo, insert hook in next ch sp, yo, draw lp through, yo, draw through 2 lps on hook; repeat from * 2 more times in same ch sp, yo, draw through all 4 lps on hook.*

Rnd 8: Join green with sc in any sl st, ch 3, (cl, ch 4, cl) in next ch sp, ch 3, *sc in next sl st, ch 3, (cl, ch 4, cl) in next ch sp, ch 3; repeat from * around, join with sl st in first sc, fasten off (6 sc, 6 ch-4 sps).

Rnd 9: Join aran with sl st in any ch-4 sp, ch 3, (2 dc, ch 2, 3 dc) in same sp, ch 3, (dc, ch 3, dc) in next sc, *ch 3, (3 dc, ch 2, 3 dc) in next ch-4 sp, ch 3, (dc, ch 3, dc) in next sc; repeat from * around; to **join,** ch 1, hdc in top of ch-3.

Rnd 10: Ch 1, sc around joining hdc, ch 5, (sc, ch 5, sc) in next ch-2 sp, *ch 5, (sc in next ch-3 sp, ch 5) 3 times, (sc, ch 5, sc) in next ch-2 sp; repeat from * around to last 2 ch-3 sps, (ch 5, sc in next ch-3 sp) 2 times; to **join,** ch 2, dc in first sc.

Rnd 11: Ch 1, sc around joining dc, ch 5, sc in next ch sp, ch 5, (sc, ch 5, sc) in next ch sp, *ch 5, (sc in next ch sp, ch 5) 4 times, (sc, ch 5, sc) in next ch sp; repeat from * around to last 2 ch sps, ch 5, (sc in next ch sp, ch 5) 2 times, join with sl st in first sc, fasten off (36 ch sps).

Next Hexagon

Rnds 1-10: Repeat same rnds of First Hexagon.

Notes: *For **joining ch-5 sp,** ch 2, sl st in corresponding ch-5 sp on other Hexagon (see Joining Diagram on page 30), ch 2.*

This Hexagon is joined across one side.

Rnd 11: Ch 1, sc around joining dc, ch 5, sc in next ch sp, ch 5, *(sc, ch 5, sc) in next ch sp, ch 5, (sc in next ch sp, ch 5) 4 times; repeat from * 3 more times; joining to side of last Hexagon, (sc, joining ch-5 sp, sc) in next ch sp on this Hexagon, joining ch-5 sp, (sc in next ch sp on this Hexagon, joining ch-5 sp) 4 times, (sc, joining ch-5 sp, sc) in next ch sp on this Hexagon, ch 5, (sc in next ch sp, ch 5) 2 times, join with sl st in first sc, fasten off.

Repeat Next Hexagon 7 more times for a total of 9 Hexagons.

Second Row
First Hexagon

Rnds 1-10: Repeat same rnds of First Row First Hexagon.

Note: *This Hexagon is joined across 2 sides.*

Rnd 11: Ch 1, sc around joining dc, ch 5, sc in next ch sp, ch 5, *(sc, ch 5, sc) in next ch sp, ch 5, (sc in next ch sp, ch 5) 4 times; repeat from * 2 more times; joining to bottom of 2nd Hexagon on last row (see diagram on page 30), (sc, joining ch-5 sp, sc) in next ch sp on this Hexagon, joining ch-5 sp, (sc in next ch sp

Continued on page 30

Rose Trellis

Continued from page 28

on this Hexagon, joining ch-5 sp) 4 times, sc in next ch sp on this Hexagon, joining ch-5 sp in side of next joining ch-5 sp on last row, sc in same ch sp on this Hexagon; joining to bottom of First Hexagon on last row, joining ch-5 sp, (sc in next ch sp on this Hexagon, joining ch-5 sp) 4 times, (sc, joining ch-5 sp, sc) in next ch sp on this Hexagon, ch 5, (sc in next ch sp, ch 5) 2 times, join with sl st in first sc, fasten off.

Next Hexagon

Rnds 1-10: Repeat same rnds of First Row First Hexagon on page 28.

Note: *This Hexagon is joined across 3 sides.*

Rnd 11: Ch 1, sc around joining dc, ch 5, sc in next ch sp, ch 5, *(sc, ch 5, sc) in next ch sp, ch 5, (sc in next ch sp, ch 5) 4 times; repeat from *; joining to bottom of corresponding Hexagon on last row (see Joining Diagram), (sc, joining ch-5 sp, sc) in next ch sp on this Hexagon, joining ch-5 sp, (sc in next ch sp on this Hexagon, joining ch-5 sp) 4 times, sc in next ch sp on this Hexagon, joining ch-5 sp in side of next joining ch-5 sp on last row, sc in same ch sp on this Hexagon; joining to bottom of next Hexagon on last row, joining ch-5 sp, (sc in next ch sp on this Hexagon, joining ch-5 sp) 4 times, sc in next ch sp on this Hexagon, joining ch-5 sp in side of next joining ch-5 sp on last row, sc in same ch sp on this Hexagon; joining to side of last Hexagon on this row, joining ch-5 sp, (sc in next ch sp on this Hexagon, joining ch-5 sp) 4 times, (sc, joining ch-5 sp, sc) in next ch sp on this Hexagon, ch 5, (sc in next ch sp, ch 5) 2 times, join with sl st in first sc, fasten off.

Repeat Next Hexagon 6 more times for a total of 8 Hexagons in this row.

Third Row
First Hexagon

Note: *This Hexagon is joined across one side.*

Work same as First Row

Next Hexagon on page 28 joining to bottom of First Hexagon on last row according to diagram.

Next Hexagon

Note: *This Hexagon is joined across 3 sides.* Work same as Second Row Next Hexagon. Repeat Next Hexagon 6 more times.

Last Hexagon

Note: *This Hexagon is joined across 2 sides.*

Work same as Second Row First Hexagon on page 28 joining to Hexagons according to diagram.

Repeat Second Row and Third Row alternately 2 times each for a total of 7 rows.

Edging

Rnd 1: Working around outer edge, join aran with sc in any ch sp, ch 5, (sc in next ch sp or in next joining ch sp, ch 5) around, join with sl st in first sc.

Rnd 2: Sl st in each of next 3 chs, dc in next sc; for **picot,** ch 3, sl st in top of dc just made; dc in same st as last dc, *sl st in next ch sp, (dc, picot, dc) in next sc; repeat from * around, join with sl st in 3rd sl st, fasten off.

Joining Diagram

First Row

Second Row

Third Row

First | Next | Next | Next
First | Next | Next
First | Next | Next | Last

▲ = Joining ch-5 sp worked across one side
▲ = Joining ch-5 sp worked across 2 sides
▲ = Joining ch-5 sp worked across 3 sides

Continued from page 27

Note: *This Hexagon is joined across 3 sides.*

Rnd 6: Ch 1, sc in first st, ch 5, skip next 2 sts, *(sc, ch 5, sc) in next ch sp, ch 5, skip next 2 sts, (sc in next st, ch 5, skip next 2 sts) 2 times; repeat from *; joining to bottom of Next Hexagon on last row (see diagram), (sc, joining ch-5 sp, sc) in next ch sp on this Hexagon, joining ch-5 sp, skip next 2 sts on this Hexagon, (sc in next st, joining ch-5 sp, skip next 2 sts on this Hexagon) 2 times, sc in next ch sp, joining ch-5 sp in side of next joining ch-5 sp on last row, sc in same ch sp on this Hexagon; joining to bottom of Next Hexagon on last row, joining ch-5 sp, skip next 2 sts on this Hexagon, (sc in next st, joining ch-5 sp, skip next 2 sts on this Hexagon) 2 times, sc in next ch sp, joining ch-5 sp in side of next joining ch-5 sp, sc in same ch sp on this Hexagon; joining to side of last Hexagon on this row, joining ch-5 sp, skip next 2 sts on this Hexagon, (sc in next st, joining ch-5 sp, skip next 2 sts on this Hexagon) 2 times, (sc, joining ch-5 sp, sc) in next ch sp, ch 5, skip next 2 sts, sc in next st, ch 5, skip last 2 sts, join with sl st in first sc, fasten off.

Repeat Next Hexagon 5 more times for a total of 7 Hexagons.

Third Row
First Hexagon

Note: *This Hexagon is joined across one side.*

Joining to bottom of First Hexagon on last row, work same as First Row Next Hexagon on page 27.

Next Hexagon

Note: *This Hexagon is joined across 3 sides.*

Work same as Second Row Next Hexagon on page 27.

Repeat Next Hexagon 6 more times for a total of 8 Hexagons.

Last Hexagon

Note: *This Hexagon is joined across 2 sides.*

Work same as Second Row First Hexagon on page 27.

Repeat Second Row and Third Row alternately 2 times each, ending with a total of 7 rows.

Joining Diagram

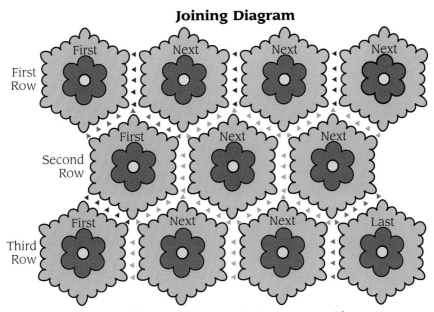

▲ = Joining ch-5 sp worked across one side
▲ = Joining ch-5 sp worked across 2 sides
▴ = Joining ch-5 sp worked across 3 sides

Symphonies

Surround yourself with masterfully composed renditions of color and texture, harmoniously blended in an album of exceptional quality. Filled with a lyrical magic all their own, you'll thrill to the ageless refrains begun by artisans of yesteryear. Orchestrate your own medley of inviting comfort as you perform the graceful waltz of hook and yarn, creating a chorus of unforgettable designs.

Shells in Song

Designed by JoHanna Dzikowski

Finished Size: 49" x 53½".

Materials: Worsted-weight yarn — 38 oz. off-white; H crochet hook or size needed to obtain gauge.

Gauge: Rows 1-2 of Strip = 2". Each Strip is 4¾" wide.

Skill Level: ★★★ Advanced

Strip
(make 10)

Row 1: Ch 6, sl st in first ch to form ring, ch 4, 8 tr in ring, turn (9 tr).

Row 2: Ch 4, dc in next st, (ch 1, dc in next st) 7 times, turn (9 dc, 8 ch-1 sps).

Row 3: Ch 1, sc in first dc, (ch 3, sc in next dc) 7 times, ch 3, sc in 3rd ch of ch-4, turn (9 sc, 8 ch-3 sps).

Row 4: Skip first 2 ch sps, 10 tr in next ch sp, skip next ch sp, sc in next ch sp leaving remaining ch sps unworked, turn (10 tr, 1 sc).

Row 5: Ch 3, skip next tr, dc in next tr, (ch 1, dc in next tr) 8 times, turn (9 dc, 8 ch-1 sps, 1 ch-3 sp).

Row 6: Ch 1, sc in first dc, (ch 3, sc in next dc) 8 times, ch 3, sc in last ch-3 sp, sc in same ch-3 sp as last sc on row before last, turn (11 sc, 9 ch-3 sps).

Row 7: Ch 3, skip next ch sp, 10 tr in next ch sp, skip next ch sp, sc in next ch sp leaving remaining ch sps unworked, turn (10 tr, 1 ch-3 sp, 1 sc).

Row 8: Ch 3, skip next tr, dc in next tr, (ch 1, dc in next tr) 8 times, ch 1, sc in same ch sp as last sc on row before last, turn (9 dc, 9 ch-1 sps, 1 ch-3 sp, 1 sc).

Row 9: Skip first sc, sc in next dc, (ch 3, sc in next dc) 8 times, ch 3, sc in next ch-3 sp, sc in same sp as last sc on row before last, turn (11 sc, 9 ch-3 sps).

Rows 10–75: Repeat rows 7–9 consecutively. At end of last row, fasten off.

Holding Strips side by side, matching wave pattern, sew long edges of Strips together loosely.

Border

Rnd 1: Join with sc in any ch-3 sp on top end of Afghan, 2 sc in same sp, 3 sc in each ch-3 sp and 2 sc in each indentation around to bottom end of Afghan, sc in end of each sc row, 2 sc in end of each dc row, 3 sc in end of each tr row and 2 sc in each ring around bottom, 3 sc in each ch-3 sp and 2 sc in each indentation across, join with sl st in first sc.

Rnd 2: Ch 1, sc in each st around with (sc next 2 sts tog) in each indentation, join.

Rnd 3: Ch 1, sc in each of first 2 sts, ch 2, (sc in each of next 2 sts, ch 2) around to last one or 2 sts, sc in last one or 2 sts, ch 2, join, fasten off. ✎

Soothing Lullaby

Designed by Josie Rabier

Finished Size: 35" x 40".

Materials: Worsted-weight yarn — 29 oz. winter white; I crochet hook or size needed to obtain gauge.

Gauge: 2 shells and 2 sc = 4"; 3 shell rows and 3 sc rows = 3¾".

Skill Level: ★★ Average

Afghan

*Notes: For **beginning half shell (beg half shell),** ch 3, 2 dc in same st.*

*For **ending half shell (end half shell),** 3 dc in last st.*

*For **shell,** 5 dc in next st.*

*For **cluster (cl),** yo 2 times, insert hook in next st, yo, draw lp through, (yo, draw through 2 lps on hook) 2 times, *yo 2 times, insert hook in same st, yo, draw lp through, (yo, draw through 2 lps on hook) 2 times; repeat from * 3 more times, yo, draw through all 6 lps on hook. Push to right side of work.*

Front of row 1 is right side of work.

Row 1: Ch 106, 2 dc in 4th ch from hook, skip next 2 chs, sc in next ch, skip next 2 chs, (shell in next ch, skip next 2 chs, sc in next ch, skip next 2 chs) across to last ch, 3 dc in last ch, turn (17 sc, 16 shells, 2 half shells).

Row 2: Ch 1, sc in first st, ch 3, cl in next sc, ch 3, (sc in 3rd dc of next shell, ch 3, cl in next sc, ch 3) across to last half shell, skip next 2 sts, sc in last st, turn (34 ch-3 sps, 18 sc, 17 cls).

Row 3: Beg half shell, sc in next cl, (shell in next sc, sc in next cl) across to last sc, end half shell in last sc, turn.

Rows 4-11: Repeat rows 2 and 3 alternately.

Row 12: Ch 1, sc in first st, (ch 3, cl in next sc, ch 3, sc in 3rd dc of next shell) 3 times, shell in next sc, (sc in 3rd dc of next shell, shell in next sc) 10 times, (sc in 3rd dc of next shell, ch 3, cl in next sc, ch 3) 3 times, sc in last st, turn (18 sc, 12 ch-3 sps, 11 shells, 6 cls).

Row 13: Beg half shell, (sc in next cl, shell in next sc) 3 times, sc in 3rd dc of next shell, (shell in next sc, sc in 3rd dc of next shell) 10 times, (shell in next sc, sc in next cl) 3 times, end half shell in last sc, turn (17 sc, 16 shells, 2 half shells).

Rows 14-51: Repeat rows 12 and 13 alternately.

Rows 52-62: Repeat rows 2 and 3 alternately, ending with row 2. At end of last row, fasten off.

Row 63: Working in starting ch on opposite side of row 1, with back of row 1 facing you, join with sc in first ch, (ch 3, cl in same ch as next cl, ch 3, sc in same ch as next shell) across, turn (17 cls, 18 sc).

Rnd 64: Working around entire outer edge, ch 4, (tr, 3 dc) in same sc, skip next ch sp, sc in next cl, (shell in next sc, sc in next cl) across to last sc, end half shell in last sc; [working in end of rows, ch 4, tr in top of last dc on end half shell just made, *sl st in sc at end of next cl row, (ch 4, tr) in same sc row, skip next shell row; repeat from * across to last cl row], (sl st, ch 4, tr, 3 dc) in next corner sc, sc in next cl, (shell in next sc, sc in next cl) across to last corner sc, end half shell in last corner sc; repeat between [ ], (sl st, ch 4, tr) in last sc row, join with sl st in top of ch-3, fasten off. ✍

Lavender Echoes

Designed by Dorris Brooks

Finished Size: 47½" x 62".

Materials: Worsted-weight yarn — 29 oz. lt. plum, 12 oz. med. plum and 8 oz. dk. plum; I crochet hook or size needed to obtain gauge.

Gauge: Row 1 of Strip = 3¾"; 5 dc rows = 3". Each Strip is 6¾" wide.

Skill Level: ★★ Average

Strip
(make 7)

Row 1: With lt. plum, ch 14, dc in 4th ch from hook, dc in each of next 3 chs, ch 2, skip next 2 chs, dc in last 5 chs, turn (10 dc, 1 ch-2 sp).

Notes: *For **front post stitch (fp)**, yo, insert hook from front to back around post of next st (see page 159), yo, draw lp through, (yo, draw through 2 lps on hook) 2 times.*

*For **back post stitch (bp)**, yo, insert hook from back to front around post of next st, yo, draw lp through, (yo, draw through 2 lps on hook) 2 times.*

Front of row 1 is wrong side of work.

Row 2: Ch 3, dc in next st, fp around next st, skip next 2 sts, 6 dc in next ch sp, skip next 2 sts, fp around next st, dc in each of last 2 sts, turn (10 dc, 2 fp).

Row 3: Ch 3, dc in next st, bp around next st, dc in each of next 2 sts, ch 2, skip next 2 sts, dc in each of next 2 sts, bp around next st, dc in each of last 2 sts, turn (8 dc, 2 bp, 1 ch-2 sp).

Rows 4-93: Repeat rows 2 and 3 alternately. At end of last row, fasten off.

Note: *For **long double crochet (ldc)**, working around posts of 2 dc on end of next row, yo, insert hook in end of next row, yo, draw up long lp, (yo, draw through 2 lps on hook) 2 times.*

Rnd 94: Working around outer edge, in ends of rows, with right side facing you, join med. plum with sl st in last row, ch 3, 2 dc in same row, (ldc, 3 dc in next row) across; working in starting ch on opposite side of row 1, ch 3, (4 tr, ch 2, 4 tr) in center ch-2 sp, ch 3; working in ends of rows, 3 dc in next row, (ldc, 3 dc in next row) across, ch 3, (4 tr, ch 2, 4 tr) in center ch-2 sp on last row, ch 3, join with sl st in top of ch-3, fasten off (92 ldc, 4 ch-3 sps, 2 ch-2 sps).

Rnd 95: Join dk. plum with sl st in 2nd tr before ch-2 sp on one end, ch 3, *(4 tr, ch 2, 4 tr) in next ch-2 sp, skip next 2 sts, dc in next st, (3 dc, ch 2, 3 dc) in next ch-3 sp, 3 dc in each of next 46 ldc skipping 3-dc groups in between, (3 dc, ch 2, 3 dc) in next ch-2 sp, skip next st*, dc in next st; repeat between **, join, fasten off (152 dc, 8 tr and 2 ch-2 sps on each long edge between end ch-2 sps).

Rnd 96: Join lt. plum with sc in first st, (sc, ch 2, 2 sc) in same st, *skip next st, sc in next st, (2 sc, ch 2, 2 sc) in next ch sp, skip next 2 sts, sc in next st, skip next st, (2 sc, ch 2, 2 sc) in next st, skip next st, sc in next st, (2 sc, ch 2, 2 sc) in next ch sp, sc in each st across to next ch sp, (2 sc, ch 2, 2 sc) in next ch sp, skip next st, sc in next st, skip next st*, (2 sc, ch 2, 2 sc) in next st; repeat between **, join with sl st in first sc, fasten off.

To **join Strips,** holding 2 Strips right sides together, working through both thicknesses across long edges, join lt. plum with sc in first corner ch sp, (ch 3, skip next 3 sts, sc in next st) across to 4 sts before last corner ch sp, ch 3, skip next 4 sts, sc in last corner ch sp, fasten off.

Join remaining Strips in same manner. ✑

Gentle Serenade

Designed by Josie Rabier

Finished Size: 31½" x 32".

Materials: Worsted-weight yarn — 29 oz. peach; H crochet hook or size needed to obtain gauge.

Gauge: 7 post sts = 2"; 9 post st rows = 4".

Skill Level: ★★ Average

Afghan

Row 1: Ch 109, dc in 4th ch from hook, dc in each ch across, turn (107 dc).

*Notes: For **back post stitch (bp),** yo, insert hook from back to front around post of next st, (see page 159), yo, draw lp through, (yo, draw through 2 lps on hook) 2 times.*

*For **front post stitch (fp),** yo, insert hook from front to back around post of next st, yo, draw lp through, (yo, draw through 2 lps on hook) 2 times.*

Beginning ch-3 is used and counted as first st.

Row 2: Ch 3, bp around next st, (fp around next st, bp around next st) across to last st, dc in last st, turn.

Row 3: Ch 3, fp around next st, (bp around next st, fp around next st) across to last st, dc in last st, turn.

Row 4: Ch 3, bp around next st, (fp around next st, bp around next st) across to last st, dc in last st, turn.

Rows 5-6: Repeat rows 3 and 4.

*Note: For **cluster (cl),** yo, insert hook in next st or ch, yo, draw lp through, yo, draw through 2 lps on hook, (yo, insert hook in same st or ch, yo, draw lp through, yo, draw through 2 lps on hook) 2 times, yo, draw through all 4 lps on hook.*

Row 7: Ch 3, fp around next st, (bp around next st, fp around next st) 5 times, ch 2, cl in next st, ch 1, skip next 2 sts, *fp around next st, (bp around next st, fp around next st) 2 times, ch 2, cl in next st, ch 1, skip next 2 sts; repeat from * 9 more times, fp around next st, (bp around next st, fp around next st) 5 times, dc in last st, turn (74 sts, 11 cls, 11 ch-2 sps, 11 ch-1 sps).

Row 8: Ch 3, bp around next st, (fp around next st, bp around next st) 5 times, ch 2, cl in next ch, ch 1, skip next ch-2 sp, *bp around next st, (fp around next st, bp around next st) 2 times, ch 2, cl in next ch, ch 1, skip next ch-2 sp; repeat from * 9 more times, bp around next st, (fp around next st, bp around next st) 5 times, dc in last st, turn.

Row 9: Ch 3, fp around next st, (bp around next st, fp around next st) 5 times, ch 2, cl in next ch, ch 1, skip next ch-2 sp, *fp around next st, (bp around next st, fp around next st) 2 times, ch 2, cl in next ch, ch 1, skip next ch-2 sp; repeat from * 9 more times, fp around next st, (bp around next st, fp around next st) 5 times, dc in last st, turn.

Rows 10-65: Repeat rows 8 and 9 alternately.

Row 66: Ch 3, bp around next st, (fp around next st, bp around next st) 5 times, dc in next ch-1 sp, dc in next cl, dc in next ch-2 sp, *bp around next st, (fp around next st, bp around next st) 2 times, dc in next ch-1 sp, dc in next cl, dc in next ch-2 sp; repeat from * 9 more times, bp around next st, (fp around next st, bp around next st) 5 times, dc in last st, turn (107 sts).

Rows 67-71: Repeat rows 3 and 4 alternately, ending with row 3. At end of last row, **do not** turn.

*Note: For **scallop,** (sl st, ch 3, dc) in next st.*

Rnd 72: For **edging,** working around outer edge, ch 3, dc in last st on last row; *working in ends of rows, skip first row, (scallop in next row, skip next row) across*; working in starting ch on opposite side of row 1, scallop in first ch; working in sps between sts, skip next 3 sts, (scallop in sp between last st and next st, skip next 3 sts) 34 times, scallop in last ch; repeat between **, scallop in next st; working in sps between sts, skip next 3 sts, (scallop in sp between last st and next st, skip next 3 sts) 34 times, join with sl st in same st as first ch-3, fasten off.

Lyrical Waves

Designed by Maggie Weldon

Finished Size: 55" x 68".

Materials: Worsted-weight yarn — 50 oz. lt. aqua and 8 oz. med. aqua; tapestry needle; J crochet hook or size needed to obtain gauge.

Gauge: 3 dc = 1"; rows 1-4 = 2¼". Each Strip is 6" wide.

Skill Level: ★★ Average

Strip
(make 9)

Row 1: With lt. aqua, ch 6, sc in 2nd ch from hook, sc in each ch across, turn (5 sc).

Row 2: Ch 4, skip next st, 5 tr in next st, ch 1, skip next st, dc in last st, turn (5 tr, 2 dc, 2 ch-1 sps).

Note: For **cluster (cl)**, *yo 2 times, insert hook from front to back around post of next tr (see page 159), yo, draw lp through, (yo, draw through 2 lps on hook) 2 times; repeat from * 4 more times, yo, draw through all 6 lps on hook.*

Row 3: Ch 4, cl, ch 1, dc in 3rd ch of last ch-4, turn (2 dc, 2 ch-1 sps, 1 cl).

Row 4: Ch 1, sc in each st and in each ch-1 sp across, turn (5 sc).

Row 5: Ch 1, sc in each st across, turn.

Rows 6-112: Repeat rows 2-5 consecutively, ending with row 4. At end of last row, **do not** fasten off.

Rnd 113: Working around outer edge, ch 3, (dc, ch 2, 2 dc) in same st, dc in each of next 3 sts, (2 dc, ch 2, 2 dc) in last st; *working in end of rows, skip first sc row, 2 dc in each dc row and dc in each sc row across to last sc row, skip last sc row*; working in starting ch on opposite side of row 1, (2 dc, ch 2, 2 dc) in first ch, dc in each of next 3 chs, (2 dc, ch 2, 2 dc) in last ch; repeat between **, join with sl st in top of ch-3, fasten off (7 dc on each short end between corner ch-2 sps, 170 dc on each long edge between corner ch-2 sps).

Rnd 114: Join med. aqua with sc in first corner ch sp, 2 sc in same sp, *(ch 1, skip next 2 sts, 2 sc in next st) 2 times, ch 1, skip next st, 3 sc in next corner ch sp, ch 1, skip next 2 sts, 2 sc in next st, (skip next st, 2 sc in next st) 83 times, ch 1, skip next st*, 3 sc in next corner ch sp; repeat between **, join with sl st in first sc, fasten off.

Rnd 115: Join lt. aqua with sl st in 2nd st, ch 3, (dc, ch 2, 2 dc) in same sp; *working over last rnd, into skipped sts on rnd before last, skip next st, 2 dc in next st, skip next 2 sts, 3 dc in next st, skip next st, 2 dc in next st, (2 dc, ch 2, 2 dc) in center corner st on last rnd; working over sts on last rnd, into skipped sts on rnd before last, (skip next st, 2 dc in next st) 85 times*, (2 dc, ch 2, 2 dc) in center corner st on last rnd; repeat between **, join with sl st in top of ch-3 (11 dc on each short end between corner ch-2 sps, 174 dc on each long edge between corner ch-2 sps).

Rnd 116: Ch 3, dc in each st around with (2 dc, ch 2, 2 dc) in each corner ch sp, join, fasten off (15 dc on each short end between corner ch-2 sps, 178 dc on each long edge between corner ch-2 sps).

Holding Strips wrong sides together, matching sts, sew long edges together through **back lps** only.

Edging
Note: For **shell**, (sc, dc, sc) in next st or sp.

Working around entire outer edge, join med. aqua with sc in first corner ch sp before one short end, (3 dc, sc) in same sp, working in sps between sts and skipping seams, *(skip next sp, shell in next sp) across to next corner ch sp, (sc, 3 dc, sc) in corner ch sp; repeat from * 2 more times, (skip next sp, shell in next sp) across, join with sl st in first sc, fasten off. ✎

Sunlight's Refrain

Designed by Lucia Biunno

Finished Size: 53" x 54" not including Fringe.

Materials: Worsted-weight yarn — 48 oz. gold; tapestry needle; H crochet hook or size needed to obtain gauge.

Gauge: 7 dc = 2"; 2 dc rows = 1".

Skill Level: ★★ Average

Center Panel

Row 1: Ch 87, dc in 4th ch from hook, dc in each of next 2 chs, (*ch 3, skip next ch, sc in next ch, ch 3, skip next ch, dc in each of next 3 chs, ch 3, skip next ch, sc in next ch, ch 3, skip next ch*, dc in next 8 chs) 4 times; repeat between **, dc in last 4 chs, turn (55 dc, 20 ch-3 sps, 10 sc).

Notes: For **front post stitch (fp)**, yo, insert hook from front to back around post of next st (see page 159), yo, draw lp through, (yo, draw through 2 lps on hook) 2 times.

For **back post stitch (bp),** yo, insert hook from back to front around post of next st, yo, draw lp through, (yo, draw through 2 lps on hook) 2 times.

Front of row 1 is wrong side of work.

Row 2: Ch 3, dc in next st, fp around next st, dc in next st, (*ch 1, dc next 2 ch sps tog, ch 1, dc in each of next 3 sts, ch 1, dc next 2 ch sps tog, ch 1*, dc in next st, fp around next st, dc in next 4 sts, fp around next st, dc in next st) 4 times; repeat between **, dc in next st, fp around next st, dc in each of last 2 sts, turn (55 dc, 20 ch-1 sps, 10 fp).

Row 3: Ch 3, dc in next st, bp around next st, dc in next st, (*ch 3, sc in next st, ch 3, dc in each of next 3 sts, ch 3, sc in next st, ch 3*, dc in next st, bp around next st, dc in each next 4 sts, bp around next st, dc in next st) 4 times; repeat between **, dc in next st, bp around next st, dc in each of last 2 sts, turn (45 dc, 20 ch-3 sps, 10 bp, 10 sc).

Rows 4-108: Repeat rows 2 and 3 alternately, ending with row 2. At end of last row, fasten off.

Side Panel
(make 2)

Row 1: Ch 55, dc in 4th ch from hook, dc in next 5 chs, *[skip next ch, (dc, ch 1, dc) in next ch, skip next ch], dc in next 15 chs; repeat from *; repeat between [ ], dc in last 7 chs, turn (50 dc, 3 ch-1 sps).

Note: Front of row 1 is wrong side of work.

Row 2: Ch 3, dc in next 5 sts, *[skip next st, fp around next st, (dc, ch 1, dc) in next ch sp, fp around next st, skip next st], dc in next 13 sts; repeat from *; repeat between [ ], dc in last 6 sts, turn (44 dc, 6 fp, 3 ch-1 sps).

Row 3: Ch 3, dc in next 4 sts, *[skip next st, bp around next st, skip next st, (2 dc, ch 1, 2 dc) in next ch sp, skip next st, bp around next st, skip next st], dc in next 11 sts; repeat from *; repeat between [ ], dc in last 5 sts, turn.

Row 4: Ch 3, dc in each of next 3 sts, *[skip next st, fp around next st, skip next 2 sts, (3 dc, ch 1, 3 dc) in next ch sp, skip next 2 sts, fp around next st, skip next st], dc in next 9 sts; repeat from *; repeat between [ ], dc in last 4 sts, turn.

Row 5: Ch 3, dc in each of next 2 sts, *[skip next st, bp around next st, skip next 3 sts, (4 dc, ch 1, 4 dc) in next ch sp, skip next 3 sts, bp around next st, skip next st], dc in next 7 sts; repeat from *; repeat between [ ], dc in each of last 3 sts, turn.

Row 6: Ch 3, dc in next 6 sts, *[skip next st, (dc, ch 1, dc) in next ch sp, skip next st], dc in next 15 sts; repeat from *; repeat between [ ], dc in last 7 sts, turn (50 dc, 3 ch-1 sps).

Row 7: Ch 3, dc in next 5 sts, *[skip next st, bp around next st, (dc, ch 1, dc) in next ch sp, bp around next st, skip next st], dc in next 13 sts; repeat from *; repeat between [ ], dc in last 6 sts, turn (44 dc, 6 bp, 3 ch-1 sps).

Row 8: Ch 3, dc in next 4 sts, *[skip next st, fp around next st, skip next st, (2 dc, ch 1, 2 dc) in next ch sp, skip next st, fp around next

Continued on page 49

Classical Harmony

Designed by Erma Fielder

Finished Size: 43" x 52" not including Fringe.

Materials: Worsted-weight yarn — 77 oz. aran; J crochet hook or size needed to obtain gauge.

Gauge: 7 dc = 2"; rows 1-2 = 1".

Skill Level: ★★★★ Challenging

Afghan

Row 1: Ch 145, sc in 2nd ch from hook, sc in each ch across, turn (144 sc).

Row 2: Ch 3, dc in each st across, turn.

Notes: *For **popcorn (pc)**, 5 dc in next st, drop lp from hook, insert hook in first st of 5-dc group, pick up dropped lp, draw through st.*

*For **double crochet front post stitch (dc fp)**, yo, insert hook from front to back around post of next st (see page 159), yo, draw lp through, (yo, draw through 2 lps on hook) 2 times.*

*For **double crochet back post stitch (dc bp)**, yo, insert hook from back to front around post of next st, yo, draw lp through, (yo, draw through 2 lps on hook) 2 times.*

*For **treble crochet front post stitch (tr fp)**, yo 2 times, insert hook from front to back around post of next st, yo, draw lp through, (yo, draw through 2 lps on hook) 3 times.*

*For **treble crochet back post stitch (tr bp)**, yo 2 times, insert hook from back to front around post of next st, yo, draw lp through, (yo, draw through 2 lps on hook) 3 times.*

Row 3: Ch 3, [*dc bp around each of next 2 sts, skip next st, tr fp around next st; working behind last st made, dc in skipped st, skip next st, dc in next st; working in front of last st made, tr fp around skipped st, dc bp around each of next 2 sts*, pc; repeat between **], ◊dc in next 4 sts, skip next st, tr fp around next st; working behind last st made, dc in skipped st, dc fp around next st, skip next st, dc in next st; working in front of last st made, tr fp around skipped st, dc in next 4 sts◊; repeat between [ ], (skip next 2 sts, tr fp around each of next 2 sts; working behind last 2 sts made, dc in each of 2 skipped sts, skip next 2 sts, dc in each of next 2 sts; working in front of last 2 sts made, tr fp around each of 2 skipped sts) 6 times; repeat between [ ]; repeat between ◊◊; repeat between [ ], dc in last st, turn.

Row 4: Ch 3, [*dc fp around each of next 2 sts, dc bp around next st, dc in each of next 2 sts, dc bp around next st, dc fp around each of next 2 sts*, ch 1, skip next pc; repeat between **], ◊dc in next 4 sts, dc bp around next st, (dc in next st, dc bp around next st) 2 times, dc in next 4 sts◊; repeat between [ ], dc bp around each of next 2 sts, dc in next 4 sts, (dc bp around next 4 sts, dc in next 4 sts) 5 times, dc bp around each of next 2 sts; repeat between [ ]; repeat between ◊◊; rcpeat between [ ], dc in last st, turn.

Row 5: Ch 3, [*dc bp around each of next 2 sts, skip next st, tr fp around next st; working behind last st made, dc in skipped st, skip next st, dc in next st; working in front of last st made, tr fp around skipped st, dc bp around each of next 2 sts*, pc in next ch sp; repeat between **], ◊dc in each of next 3 sts, skip next st, tr fp around next st; working behind last st made, dc in skipped st, dc in next st, dc fp around next st, dc in next st, skip next st, dc in next st; working in front of last st made, tr fp around skipped st, dc in each of next 3 sts◊; repeat between [ ], (skip next 2 sts, dc in each of next 2 sts; working in front of last 2 sts made, tr fp around each of 2 skipped sts, skip next 2 sts, tr fp around each of next 2 sts; working behind last 2 sts made, dc in each of 2 skipped sts) 6 times; repeat between [ ]; repeat between ◊◊; repeat between [ ], dc in last st, turn.

Row 6: Ch 3, [*dc fp around each of next 2 sts, dc bp around next st, dc in each of next 2 sts, dc bp around next st, dc fp around each of next 2 sts*, ch 1, skip next pc; repeat between **], ◊dc in each of next 3 sts, dc bp around next st, (dc in each of next 2 sts, dc bp around

Continued on page 48

Continued from page 46

next st) 2 times, dc in each of next 3 sts◊; repeat between [ ], dc in each of next 2 sts, dc bp around next 4 sts, (dc in next 4 sts, dc bp around next 4 sts) 5 times, dc in each of next 2 sts; repeat between [ ]; repeat between ◊◊; repeat between [ ], dc in last st, turn.

Row 7: Ch 3, [*dc bp around each of next 2 sts, skip next st, tr fp around next st; working behind last st made, dc in skipped st, skip next st, dc in next st; working in front of last st made, tr fp around skipped st, dc bp around each of next 2 sts*, pc in next ch sp; repeat between **], ◊dc in each of next 2 sts, skip next st, tr fp around next st; working behind last st made, dc in skipped st, dc in each of next 2 sts, dc fp around next st, dc in each of next 2 sts, skip next st, dc in next st; working in front of last st made, tr fp around next st, dc in each of skipped 2 sts◊; repeat between [ ], (skip next 2 sts, tr fp around each of next 2 sts; working behind last 2 sts made, dc in each of 2 skipped sts, skip next 2 sts, dc in each of next 2 sts; working in front of last 2 sts made, tr fp around each of 2 skipped sts) 6 times; repeat between [ ]; repeat between ◊◊; repeat between [ ], dc in last st, turn.

Row 8: Ch 3, [*dc fp around each of next 2 sts, dc bp around next st, dc in each of next 2 sts, dc bp around next st, dc fp around each of next 2 sts*, ch 1, skip next pc; repeat between **], ◊dc in each of next 2 sts, dc bp around next st, (dc in each of next 3 sts, dc bp around next st) 2 times, dc in each of next 2 sts◊; repeat between [ ]; dc bp around each of next 2 sts, dc in next 4 sts, (dc bp around next 4 sts, dc in next 4 sts) 5 times, dc bp around each of next 2 sts; repeat between [ ]; repeat between ◊◊; repeat between [ ], dc in last st, turn.

Row 9: Ch 3, [*dc bp around each of next 2 sts, skip next st, tr fp around next st; working behind last st made, dc in skipped st, skip next st, dc in next st; working in front of last st, tr fp around skipped st, dc bp around each of next 2 sts*, pc in next ch sp; repeat between **], ◊dc in next st, skip next st, tr fp around next st; working behind last st made, dc in skipped st,

dc in each of next 3 sts, dc fp around next st, dc in each of next 3 sts, skip next st, dc in next st; working in front of last st made, tr fp around skipped st, dc in next st◊; repeat between [ ], (skip next 2 sts, dc in each of next 2 sts; working in front of last 2 sts made, tr fp around each of 2 skipped sts, skip next 2 sts, tr fp around each of next 2 sts; working behind last 2 sts made, dc in each of 2 skipped sts) 6 times; repeat between [ ]; repeat between ◊◊; repeat between [ ], dc in last st, turn.

Row 10: Ch 3, [*dc fp around each of next 2 sts, dc bp around next st, dc in each of next 2 sts, dc bp around next st, dc fp around each of next 2 sts*, ch 1, skip next pc; repeat between **], ◊dc in next st, dc bp around next st, (dc in next 4 sts, dc bp around next st) 2 times, dc in next st◊; repeat between [ ], dc in each of next 2 sts, dc bp around next 4 sts, (dc in next 4 sts, dc bp around next 4 sts) 5 times, dc in each of next 2 sts; repeat between [ ]; repeat between ◊◊; repeat between [ ], dc in last st, turn.

Row 11: Ch 3, [*dc bp around each of next 2 sts, skip next st, tr fp around next st; working behind last st made, dc in skipped st, skip next st, dc in next st; working in front of last st made, tr fp around skipped st, dc bp around each of next 2 sts*, pc in next ch sp; repeat between **], ◊skip next st, tr fp around next st; working behind last st made, dc in skipped st, dc in each of next 2 sts, skip next st, tr fp around next st; working behind last st made, dc in skipped st, dc fp around next st, skip next st, dc in next st; working in front of last st made, tr fp around skipped st, dc in each of next 2 sts, skip next st, dc in next st; working in front of last st made, tr fp around skipped st◊; repeat between [ ], (skip next 2 sts, tr fp around each of next 2 sts; working behind last 2 sts made, dc in each of 2 skipped sts, skip next 2 sts, dc in each of next 2 sts; working in front of last 2 sts made, tr fp around each of 2 skipped sts) 6 times; repeat between [ ]; repeat between ◊◊; repeat between [ ], dc in last st, turn.

Row 12: Ch 3, [*dc fp around each of next

2 sts, dc bp around next st, dc in each of next 2 sts, dc bp around next st, dc fp around each of next 2 sts*, ch 1, skip next pc; repeat between **], ◊dc bp around next st, dc in each of next 3 sts, dc bp around next st, (dc in next st, dc bp around next st) 2 times, dc in each of next 3 sts, dc bp around next st◊; repeat between [ ]; dc bp around each of next 2 sts, dc in next 4 sts, (dc bp around next 4 sts, dc in next 4 sts) 5 times, dc bp around each of next 2 sts; repeat between [ ]; repeat between ◊◊; repeat between [ ], dc in last st, turn.

Rows 13-114: Repeat rows 5-12 consecutively, ending with row 10.

Row 115: Ch 1, sc in each of first 3 sts, sc next 2 sts tog, (sc in each of next 3 sts, sc next 2 sts tog) across to last 4 sts, sc in last 4 sts, fasten off (116 sc).

Row 116: Working in starting ch on opposite side of row 1, with wrong side facing you, join with sc in first ch, sc in each of next 2 chs, sc next 2 chs tog, (sc in each of next 3 chs, sc next 2 chs tog) across to last 4 chs, sc in last 4 chs, fasten off.

Fringe

For **each Fringe,** cut 10 strands each 14" long. With all 10 strands held together, fold in half, insert hook in st, draw fold through, draw all loose ends through fold, tighten. Trim ends.

Fringe in first and last sts and in every (sc 2 sts tog) across each short end of Afghan.

Holding 2nd half of first Fringe and first half of next Fringe together, tie overhand knot 1" from knot on Fringes according to diagram. Holding 2nd half of last Fringe and first half of next Fringe together, tie overhand knot 1" from knot on Fringes. Repeat in same manner across leaving 2nd half of last Fringe unworked.

Sunlight's Refrain

Continued from page 44

st, skip next st], dc in next 11 sts; repeat from *; repeat between [ ], dc in last 5 sts, turn.

Row 9: Ch 3, dc in each of next 3 sts, *[skip next st, bp around next st, skip next 2 sts, (3 dc, ch 1, 3 dc) in next ch sp, skip next 2 sts, bp around next st, skip next st], dc in next 9 sts; repeat from *; repeat between [ ], dc in last 4 sts, turn.

Row 10: Ch 3, dc in each of next 2 sts, *[skip next st, fp around next st, skip next 3 sts, (4 dc, ch 1, 4 dc) in next ch sp, skip next 3 sts, fp around next st, skip next st], dc in next 7 sts; repeat from *; repeat between [ ], dc in each of last 3 sts, turn.

Row 11: Ch 3, dc in next 6 sts, *[skip next st, (dc, ch 1, dc) in next ch sp, skip next st], dc

in next 15 sts; repeat from *; repeat between [ ], dc in last 7 sts, turn (50 dc, 3 ch-1 sps).

Rows 12-108: Repeat rows 2-11 consecutively, ending with row 8. At end of last row, fasten off.

Holding one Side Panel and Center Panel right sides together, sew ends of rows together.

Repeat with remaining Side Panel.

Fringe

For **each Fringe,** cut one strand 12" long. Fold in half, insert hook in st, draw fold through st, draw all loose ends through fold, tighten. Trim ends.

Fringe in each st on short ends of Afghan.

Hearts A' Flight

Designed by Sue Childress

Finished Size: 50" x 62".

Materials: Worsted-weight yarn — 42 oz. rose; H crochet hook or size needed to obtain gauge.

Gauge: 13 dc = 4"; 7 dc rows = 4".

Skill Level: ★★ Average

Afghan

Row 1: Ch 157, dc in 4th ch from hook, dc in each ch across, turn (155 dc).

Notes: For **cluster (cl),** yo, insert hook in next ch sp, yo, draw lp through, yo, draw through 2 lps on hook, *yo, insert hook in same sp, yo, draw lp through, yo, draw through 2 lps on hook; repeat from *, yo, draw through all 4 lps on hook.

For **beginning block (beg block),** ch 3, dc in each of next 2 dc.

For **block,** dc in each of next 2 dc, or, dc in next ch sp, dc in next dc.

For **mesh,** ch 1, skip next st or ch sp, dc in next dc.

For **cl block,** cl in next ch sp, dc in next dc.

Row 2: For **row 2 of Angel Graph** (see page 55), beg block, 75 mesh, 1 block, turn (75 mesh, 2 blocks).

Rows 3-104: Work sts according to next row on graph. At end of last row, **do not** fasten off.

Border

Note: For **beginning cl (beg cl),** ch 3, *yo, insert hook in same st, yo, draw lp through, yo, draw through 2 lps on hook; repeat from *, yo, draw through all 3 lps on hook.

Rnd 1: Working around outer edge, beg cl, ch 1, cl in same st, ch 1, skip next st, (cl in next st, ch 1, skip next st) across to last st, (cl, ch 1, cl) in last st; *working in end of rows, ch 1, (cl in next row, ch 1) across*; working in starting ch on opposite side of row 1, (cl, ch 1, cl) in first ch, ch 1, skip next ch, (cl in next ch, ch 1, skip next ch) across to last ch, (cl, ch 1, cl) in last ch; repeat between **, join with sl st in top of beg cl.

Rnd 2: Sl st in next ch sp, ch 3, 6 dc in same sp, *[sc in next ch sp, (5 dc in next ch sp, sc in next ch sp) across] to next corner ch sp, 7 dc in next corner ch sp; repeat from * 2 more times; repeat between [ ], join with sl st in top of ch-3, fasten off. ✍

Graph on page 55

Ode to Pearls

Designed by Trudy Atteberry

Finished Size: 46" x 66".

Materials: Worsted-weight yarn — 32 oz. beige; K crochet hook or size needed to obtain gauge.

Gauge: Rnds 1 and 2 of Motif = 4½" across. Each Motif is 8" across.

Skill Level: ★★ Average

First Row
First Motif

Notes: *For **beginning cluster (beg cl),** ch 4, *yo 2 times, insert hook in same sp, yo, draw lp through, (yo, draw through 2 lps on hook) 2 times; repeat from *, yo, draw through all 3 lps on hook.*

*For **cluster (cl),** yo 2 times, insert hook in next ch sp, yo, draw lp through, (yo, draw through 2 lps on hook) 2 times, *yo 2 times, insert hook in same sp, yo, draw lp through, (yo, draw through 2 lps on hook) 2 times; repeat from *, yo, draw through all 4 lps on hook.*

Rnd 1: Ch 4, sl st in first ch to form ring, beg cl, ch 4, (cl in ring, ch 4) 5 times, join with sl st in top of beg cl (6 cls, 6 ch-4 sps).

Rnd 2: Ch 1, sc in first cl, *[ch 1, dc in next ch sp, (ch 1, dc in same sp) 2 times, ch 1], sc in next cl; repeat from * 4 more times; repeat between [ ], join with sl st in first sc (24 ch-1 sps).

Rnd 3: Sl st in next ch sp, sl st in next st, sl st in next ch sp, ch 1, sc in same sp, ch 3, sc in next ch sp, ch 5, skip next 2 ch sps, (sc in next ch sp, ch 3, sc in next ch sp, ch 5, skip next 2 ch sps) around, join (6 ch-3 sps, 6 ch-5 sps).

Rnd 4: Sl st in next ch-3 sp, ch 1, sc in same sp, ch 3, (cl, ch 3, cl) in next ch-5 sp, ch 3, *sc in next ch-3 sp, ch 3, (cl, ch 3, cl) in next ch-5 sp, ch 3; repeat from * around, join (18 ch-3 sps).

Rnd 5: Sl st in next ch sp, ch 1, sc in same sp, *[ch 3, (sc, ch 5, sc) in next ch sp, ch 3, sc in next ch sp, ch 5], sc in next ch sp; repeat from * 4 more times; repeat between [ ], join, fasten off (12 ch-3 sps, 12 ch-5 sps).

Second Motif

Rnds 1-4: Repeat same rnds of First Motif.

Rnd 5: Sl st in next ch sp, ch 1, sc in same sp, *ch 3, (sc, ch 5, sc) in next ch sp, ch 3, sc in next ch sp, ch 5, sc in next ch sp; repeat from * 3 more times, ch 3, sc in next ch sp; joining to bottom of last Motif made (see Assembly Diagram on page 54), ch 2, sl st in corresponding ch-5 sp on last Motif, ch 2, sc in same sp on this Motif, ch 3, sc in next ch sp, ch 2, sl st in next ch-5 sp on last Motif, ch 2, sc in next ch sp on this Motif, ch 3, sc in ncxt ch sp, ch 2, sl st in next ch-5 sp on last Motif, ch 2, sc in same sp on this Motif, ch 3, sc in next ch sp, ch 5, join, fasten off.

Repeat Second Motif 5 more times for a total of 7 Motifs.

Second Row
First Motif

Rnds 1-4: Repeat same rnds of First Row First Motif.

Rnd 5: Joining to upper side of First Motif on last row (see diagram), repeat same rnd of First Row Second Motif.

Second Motif

Rnds 1-4: Repeat same rnds of First Row First Motif.

Rnd 5: Sl st in next ch sp, ch 1, sc in same sp, *ch 3, (sc, ch 5, sc) in next ch sp, ch 3, sc in next ch sp, ch 5, sc in next ch sp; repeat from *, ch 3, sc in next ch sp; joining to bottom of last Motif made, ch 2, sl st in corresponding ch-5 sp, ch 2, sc in same sp on this Motif, ch 3, sc in next ch sp, [ch 2, sl st in next ch-5 sp on last Motif, ch 2, sc in next ch sp on this Motif, ch 3, sc in next ch sp, ch 2, sl st in next ch-5 sp on last Motif, ch 2, sc in same sp on this Motif, ch 3, sc in next ch sp]; joining to lower side of adjoining Motif on last row; repeat between [ ]; joining to upper side of next Motif on last row; repeat between [ ], ch 5, join, fasten off.

Continued from page 53

Repeat Second Motif 5 more times for a total of 7 Motifs.

Eighth Motif

Rnds 1-4: Repeat same rnds of First Row First Motif on page 53.

Rnd 5: Sl st in next ch sp, ch 1, sc in same sp, *ch 3, (sc, ch 5, sc) in next ch sp, ch 3, sc in next ch sp, ch 5, sc in next ch sp; repeat from * 2 more times, ch 3, sc in next ch sp; joining to bottom of last Motif made, ch 2, sl st in corresponding ch-5 sp on last Motif made, ch 2, sc in same sp on this Motif, ch 3, sc in next ch sp, [ch 2, sl st in next ch-5 sp on last Motif, ch 2, sc in next ch sp on this Motif, ch 3, sc in next ch sp, ch 2, sl st in next ch-5 sp on last Motif, ch 2, sc in same sp on this Motif, ch 3, sc in next ch sp]; joining to lower side of adjoining Motif; repeat between [ ], ch 5, join, fasten off.

Third Row
First Motif

Rnds 1-4: Repeat same rnds of First Row First Motif on page 53.

Rnd 5: Sl st in next ch sp, ch 1, sc in same sp, *ch 3, (sc, ch 5, sc) in next ch sp, ch 3, sc in next ch sp, ch 5, sc in next ch sp; repeat from * 2 more times, ch 3, sc in next ch sp; joining to lower side of First Motif on last row (see diagram), ch 2, sl st in corresponding ch-5 sp on last Motif, ch 2, sc in same sp on this Motif, ch 3, sc in next ch sp, [ch 2, sl st in next ch-5 sp on last Motif, ch 2, sc in next ch sp on this Motif, ch 3, sc in next ch sp, ch 2, sl st in next ch-5 sp on last Motif, ch 2, sc in same sp on this Motif, ch 3, sc in next ch sp]; joining to upper side of next Motif on last row; repeat between [ ], ch 5, join, fasten off.

Second Motif

Rnds 1-4: Repeat same rnds of First Row First Motif on page 53.

Rnd 5: Repeat same rnd of Second Row Second Motif on page 53.

Repeat Second Motif 5 more times for a total of 7 Motifs.

Repeat Second Row and Third Row alternately 2 more times for a total of 7 rows.

Edging

Working around entire outer edge, join with sc in upper right corner ch-5 sp as shown in diagram, ch 5, sc in same sp, ch 5; skipping joined ch-5 sps between Motifs, ch 5, sc in next ch-3 sp, ch 5, *(sc, ch 5, sc) in next ch-5 sp or around next joining sc, ch 5, sc in next ch-3 sp, ch 5; repeat from * around, join with sl st in first sc, fasten off. ✎

Assembly Diagram

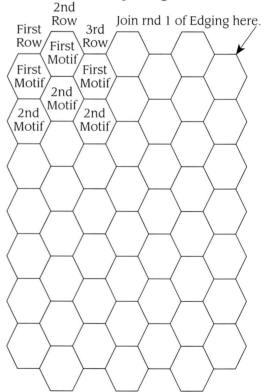

Hearts A' Flight

Instructions on page 51

Angel Graph

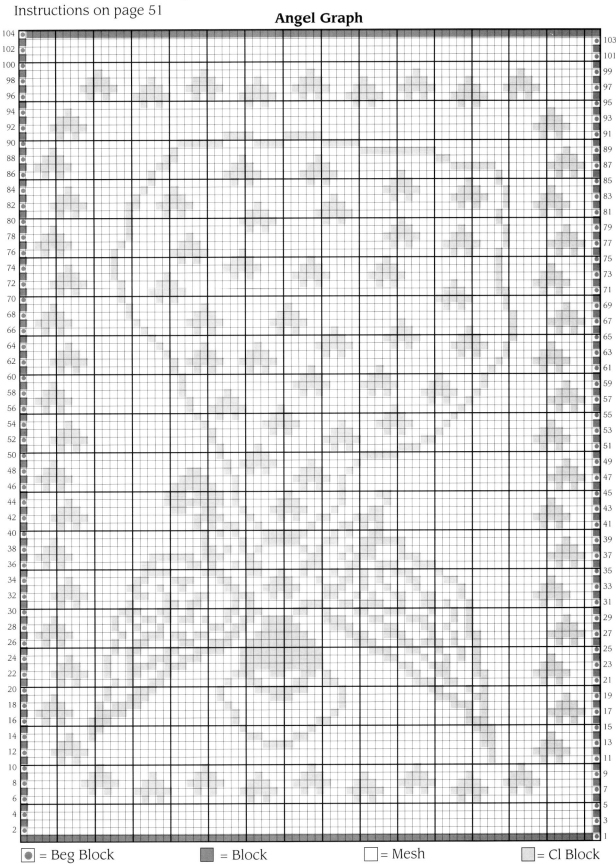

= Beg Block   = Block   = Mesh   = Cl Block

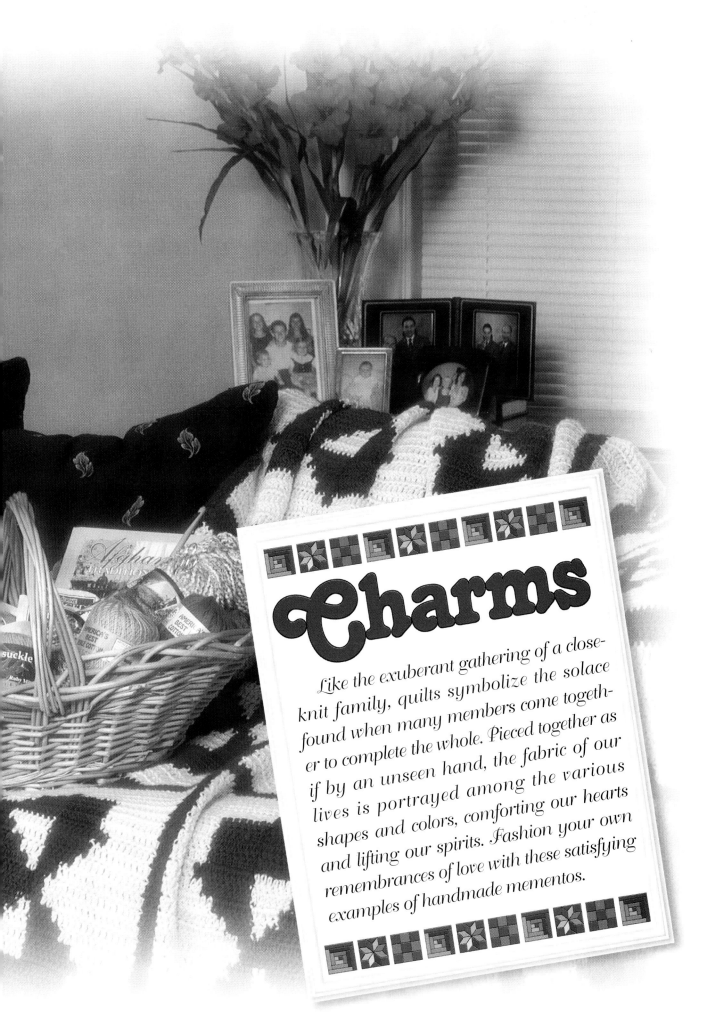

Charms

Like the exuberant gathering of a close-knit family, quilts symbolize the solace found when many members come together to complete the whole. Pieced together as if by an unseen hand, the fabric of our lives is portrayed among the various shapes and colors, comforting our hearts and lifting our spirits. Fashion your own remembrances of love with these satisfying examples of handmade mementos.

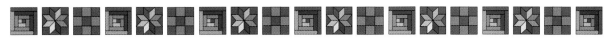

Triangle Treasure

Designed by Carol Smith

Finished Size: 49" x 65".

Materials: Worsted-weight yarn — 17½ oz. green, 14 oz. each variegated, burgundy and blue; tapestry needle, I crochet hook or size needed to obtain gauge.

Gauge: 3 dc = 1"; 3 dc rows = 2". Each Motif is 8" across long edge.

Skill Level: ★★ Average

Motif
(make 24 variegated, 24 blue, 21 burgundy, 21 green)

Row 1: Ch 4, sl st in first ch to form ring, ch 3, 2 dc in ring, turn (3 dc).

Rows 2-10: Ch 3, dc in same st, dc in each st across to last st, 2 dc in last st, turn. At end of last row (21), **do not** turn.

Rnd 11: Working around outer edge in sts and in ends of rows, ch 3, 4 dc in same st, 2 dc in each of next 10 rows, 5 dc in ring, 2 dc in each of next 10 rows, 5 dc in next st, dc in next 19 sts, join with sl st in top of ch-3, fasten off.

Holding Motifs right sides together, matching sts, with coordinating color yarn, sew together through **back lps** according to Assembly Diagram.

Border
Working around entire outer edge, join green with sl st in any st, ch 3, dc in each st and in each seam around spacing sts evenly and increasing as needed for Afghan to lay flat, join with sl st in top of ch-3, fasten off. ✏

Assembly Diagram

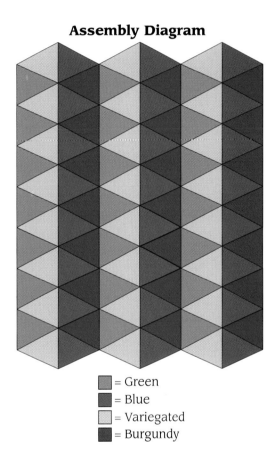

■ = Green
■ = Blue
□ = Variegated
■ = Burgundy

Ohio Star Variation

Designed by Susie Spier Maxfield

Finished Size: 51" x 72" not including Fringe.

Materials: Worsted-weight yarn — 27 oz. burgundy, 18 oz. off-white and 12 oz. purple; tapestry needle; H crochet hook or size needed to obtain gauge.

Gauge: 7 dc = 2"; 5 dc rows = 3". Each Block is 17" x 18".

Skill Level: ★★ Average

Block
(make 12)

Notes: *When changing colors (see page 159), always drop yarn to wrong side of work. Use a separate skein of yarn for each color section. **Do not** carry yarn across from one section to another. Fasten off at end of each color section.*

Work odd-numbered rows on graph from right to left and even-numbered rows from left to right.

Ch-3 at beginning of rows is used and counted as first st. Each square on graph equals 2 dc.

Row 1: With burgundy, ch 62, dc in 4th ch from hook, dc in each ch across, turn (60 dc).

Row 2: For **row 2 of Block Graph**, ch 3, dc in next st changing to off-white, dc in next 56 sts changing to burgundy in last st made, dc in each of last 2 sts, turn.

Rows 3-30: Ch 3, dc in each st across changing colors according to Block Graph, turn. At end of last row, fasten off.

Holding Blocks wrong sides together, with burgundy, sew together through **back lps** in 3 rows of 4 Blocks each.

Edging

Working around entire outer edge, join burgundy with sc in any st, sc in each st and 2 sc in end of each row around with 2 sc in each corner st, join with sl st in first sc, fasten off.

Fringe

For **each Fringe,** cut 3 strands of burgundy each 18" long. With all 3 strands held together, fold in half, insert hook in st, draw fold through, draw all loose ends through fold, tighten, trim ends.

Fringe in every other st on each short end of Afghan. ✑

Block Graph

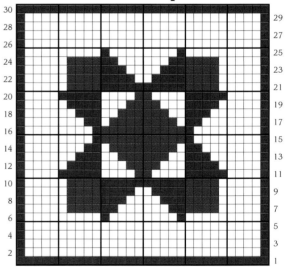

Each square on graph equals 2 dc.

■ = Burgundy
■ = Purple
☐ = Off-white

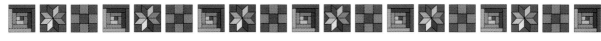

Tulip Field

Designed by Susie Spier Maxfield

Finished Size: 55½" x 86" not including Fringe.

Materials: Worsted-weight yarn — 25 oz. aran fleck, 20 oz. green fleck, 15 oz. navy fleck and 10 oz. red fleck; tapestry needle; I crochet hook or size needed to obtain gauge.

Gauge: 13 dc = 4"; 7 dc rows = 5". Each Block is 18½" x 21½".

Skill Level: ★★ Average

Block
(make 12)

Notes: *When changing colors (see page 159), always drop yarn to wrong side of work. Use a separate skein of yarn for each color section. **Do not** carry yarn across from one section to another. Fasten off at end of each color section.*

Work odd-numbered rows on graph from right to left and even-numbered rows from left to right.

Ch-3 at beginning of rows is used and counted as first st. Each square on graph equals 2 dc.

Row 1: With green fleck, ch 62, dc in 4th ch from hook, dc in each ch across, turn (60 dc).

Row 2: For **row 2 of Block Graph,** ch 3, dc in next st changing to aran fleck, dc in next 56 sts changing to green fleck in last st made, dc in each of last 2 sts, turn.

Rows 3-30: Ch 3, dc in each st across changing colors according to Block Graph, turn. At end of last row, fasten off.

Holding Blocks wrong sides together, matching sts, with green fleck, sew together in 3 rows of 4 Blocks each.

Edging

Working around entire outer edge, join green fleck with sc in any st, sc in each st and 2 sc in end of each row around with 2 sc in each corner st, join with sl st in first sc, fasten off.

Fringe

For **each Fringe,** cut 3 strands of green fleck each 18" long. With all 3 strands held together, fold in half, insert hook in st, draw fold through, draw all loose ends through fold, tighten. Trim ends.

Fringe in every other st on each short end of Afghan.

Block Graph

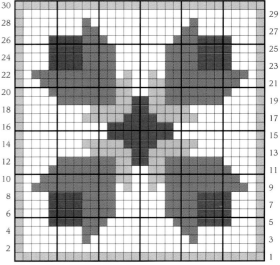

Each square equals 2 dc.

■ = Navy Fleck
□ = Aran Fleck
■ = Red Fleck
▨ = Green Fleck

Cloudy Days

Designed by Lyne Pickens

Finished Size: 34" x 37".

Materials: Sport-weight yarn — 9 oz. white and 7 oz. blue; F crochet hook or size needed to obtain gauge.

Gauge: 4 sts = 1"; 4 sc rows = 1"; rnd 1 = 1½" across. Each Motif is 2¾" square.

Skill Level: ★★ Average

Solid Motif
(make 66)

Rnd 1: With blue, ch 4, sl st in first ch to form ring, ch 3, 2 dc in ring, ch 2, (3 dc in ring, ch 2) 3 times, join with sl st in top of ch-3 (12 dc, 4 ch sps).

Rnd 2: Sl st in each of next 2 sts, sl st in next ch sp, ch 3, (2 dc, ch 2, 3 dc) in same sp, (3 dc, ch 2, 3 dc) in each ch sp around, join (24 dc, 4 ch sps).

Rnd 3: Working this rnd in **back lps** only, ch 1, sc in each of first 3 sts, sc in next ch, ch 2, sc in next ch, (sc in each st across to next corner ch-2 sp, sc in next ch, ch 2, sc in next ch) 3 times, sc in each of last 3 sts, join with sl st in first sc, fasten off.

Two-Color Motif
(make 66)

Rnd 1: With white, ch 4, sl st in first ch to form ring, ch 3, 2 dc in ring, ch 2, (3 dc in ring, ch 2) 3 times, join with sl st in top of ch-3 (12 dc, 4 ch sps).

Rnd 2: Sl st in each of next 2 sts, sl st in next ch sp, ch 3, (2 dc, ch 2, 3 dc) in same sp, (3 dc, ch 2, 3 dc) in each ch sp around, join, fasten off (24 dc, 4 ch sps).

Rnd 3: Working this rnd in **back lps** only, join blue with sc in first st after any ch sp, sc in next 5 sts, sc in next ch, ch 2, sc in next ch, (sc in each st across to next corner ch sp, sc

in next ch, ch 2, sc in next ch) around, join with sl st in first sc, fasten off.

Holding Motifs right sides together, matching sts, working through both thicknesses in **back lps** only, with blue, sl st together according to Assembly Diagram.

Border

Rnd 1: Working around outer edge, in **back lps** only, skipping seams, join white with sc in any st, sc in each st and in each ch around with (sc, ch 2, sc) in each corner ch sp, join with sl st in first sc.

Rnds 2-7: Ch 1, sc in each st around with (sc, ch 2, sc) in each corner ch sp, join.

Rnd 8: Ch 1; working from left to right, **reverse sc** (see page 159) in each st and in each ch around, join, fasten off.

Rnd 9: For **trim,** working in remaining **front lps** of Afghan, skipping seams, join white with sl st in any st, ch 1, reverse sc in each st and in each ch around, join, fasten off. ✎

Assembly Diagram

Flying Rainbows

Designed by Hazel Osborn Jones

Finished Size: 52" x 82".

Materials: Worsted-weight yarn — 42 oz. navy blue, 6 oz. each lt. peach, dk. peach and dk. orange, 3 oz. each lt. purple, dk. purple, lt. blue, med. blue, turquoise, lt. green, med. green, dk. green, lt. orange and yellow; tapestry needle; G crochet hook or size needed to obtain gauge.

Gauge: Rnds 1 and 2 = 3" across. Each Motif is 5" square.

Skill Level: ★★ Average

Corner Block

Rnd 1: With navy blue, ch 4, 2 dc in fourth ch from hook, (ch 1, 3 dc) 3 times in same ch, ch 1, join with sl st in top of ch-3 (12 dc, 4 ch-1 sps).

Rnd 2: Sl st in each of next 2 sts, sl st in next ch sp, ch 3, (2 dc, ch 1, 3 dc, ch 1) in same sp, (3 dc, ch 1, 3 dc, ch 1) in each ch sp around, join with sl st in top of ch-3.

Rnds 3-4: Sl st in each of next 2 sts, sl st in next corner ch sp, ch 3, (2 dc, ch 1, 3 dc, ch 1) in same sp, *[(3 dc, ch 1) in each ch sp across to next corner ch sp], (3 dc, ch 1, 3 dc, ch 1) in next sp; repeat from * 2 more times; repeat between [ ], join. At end of last rnd, fasten off.

Two–Color Block
(make 134—see Note)

Notes: *Work Two-Color Blocks using navy and colors indicated on Assembly Diagram (see page 73).*

When changing colors (see page 159), always drop yarn to wrong side of work. Work over dropped color as you carry it across to next section of same color.

Ch-3 at beginning of rows is used and counted as first st.

Rnd 1: With navy blue, ch 5, 3 dc in fourth ch from hook changing to next color in last st made, (ch 1, 3 dc in same ch) 2 times changing to navy blue in last st made, ch 1, 2 dc in same ch, join with sl st in top of 4th ch of ch-5 (12 dc, 4 ch-1 sps).

Rnd 2: Sl st in next ch sp, ch 3, (2 dc, ch 1, 3 dc) in same ch sp, ch 1, 3 dc in next ch sp changing to next color in last st made, ch 1, 3 dc in same sp, ch 1, (3 dc, ch 1, 3 dc) in next ch sp, 3 dc in next ch sp changing to navy blue in last st made, ch 1, 3 dc in same sp, ch 1, join with sl st in top of ch-3.

Rnds 3-4: Sl st in each of next 2 sts, sl st in next corner ch sp, ch 3, (2 dc, ch 1, 3 dc) in same sp, ch 1, (3 dc, ch 1) in each ch sp across to next corner ch sp, (3 dc in next ch sp changing to next color in last st made, ch 1, 3 dc in same sp), ch 1, (3 dc, ch 1) in each ch sp across to next corner ch sp, (3 dc, ch 1, 3 dc) in next ch sp, ch 1, (3 dc, ch 1) in each ch sp across to next corner ch sp, 3 dc in next sp changing to navy blue in last st made, ch 1, 3 dc in same sp, ch 1, (3 dc, ch 1) in each ch sp across, join. At end of last rnd, fasten off.

Holding Blocks wrong sides together, matching sts, with navy blue, sew together through **back lps** according to Assembly Diagram (see page 73).

Border

Rnd 1: Working around outer edge, join navy blue with sl st in corner ch sp before one short end, ch 3, (2 dc, ch 1, 3 dc, ch 1) in same sp, (3 dc, ch 1) in each ch sp and in each joining seam around with (3 dc, ch 1, 3 dc, ch 1) in each corner ch sp, join with sl st in top of ch-3.

Rnds 2-4: Sl st in each of next 2 sts, sl st in next corner ch sp, ch 3, (2 dc, ch 1, 3 dc, ch 1) in same sp, (3 dc, ch 1) in each ch sp around with (3 dc, ch 1, 3 dc, ch 1) in each corner ch sp, join.

Rnd 5: Sl st in each of next 2 sts, sc in next ch sp, ch 3, 3 dc in same sp, (sc, ch 3, 3 dc) in each ch sp around, join with sl st in first sc, fasten off. ✍

Assembly Diagram on page 73

Americana Star

Designed by Darla Fanton

Finished Size: 58" x 74½".

Materials: Worsted-weight yarn — 25 oz. white, 16 oz. blue and 13 oz. red; tapestry needle; H crochet hook or size needed to obtain gauge.

Gauge: 3 hdc = 1"; 3 hdc rows = 1". Each Block is 9½" x 10".

Skill Level: ★★ Average

Block
(make 35)

Notes: *When changing colors (see page 159), always drop yarn to wrong side of work. Use a separate skein of yarn for each color section.* **Do not** *carry yarn across from one section to another. Fasten off at end of each color section.*

Work odd-numbered rows on graph from right to left and even-numbered rows from left to right.

Ch-2 at beginning of rows is used and counted as first st. Each square on graph equals one hdc.

Row 1: For **row 1 of Block Graph** (see page 73), with white, ch 31, hdc in 2nd ch from hook, hdc in next 6 chs changing to blue in last st made, hdc in next ch changing to white, hdc in next 14 chs changing to red in last st made, hdc in next ch changing to white, hdc in last 7 chs, turn (30 hdc).

Rows 2-28: Ch 2, hdc in each st across changing colors according to Block Graph, turn. At end of last row, fasten off.

Holding Blocks wrong sides together, matching sts, with white, sew together in 5 rows of 7 Blocks each.

Corner Square
(make 4)

Row 1: With red, ch 11, hdc in 2nd ch from hook, hdc in each ch across, turn (10 hdc).

Rows 2-10: Ch 2, hdc in each st across, turn. At end of last row, fasten off.

Top/Bottom Strip
(make 2)

Row 1: For **row 1 of Strip Graph** (see page 73), with white, ch 11, hdc in 2nd ch from hook, hdc in next 7 chs changing to blue in last st made, hdc in next ch changing to white, hdc in last ch, turn (10 hdc).

Rows 2-30: Ch 2, hdc in each st across changing colors according to Strip Graph, turn.

Rows 31-150: Ch 2, hdc in each st across changing colors according to rows 1-30 consecutively. At end of last row, fasten off.

Holding pieces right sides together, easing to fit, with white, sew long edge of one Strip across each short end.

Side Strip
(make 2)

Row 1: Repeat same row of Top/Bottom Strip.

Rows 2-30: Repeat same rows of Top/Bottom Strip.

Rows 31-210: Ch 2, hdc in each st across changing colors according to rows 1-30 of Strip Graph consecutively. At end of last row, fasten off.

Holding right sides of Corner Square and short end of Side Strip together, matching sts, with white, sew one Square on each end of Strip.

Repeat with remaining Strip and Squares.

Holding pieces right sides together, easing to fit, with white, sew one Side Strip across each long edge.

Border

Rnd 1: Working around entire outer edge in sts and in ends of rows, skipping seams, join red with sl st in any st, ch 2, hdc in every other st or row around with 3 hdc in each corner st, join with sl st in top of ch-2.

Continued on page 73

All-American Cats

Designed by Martha Brooks Stein

Finished Size: 45" x 55".

Materials: Worsted-weight yarn — 21 oz. off-white, 10½ oz. med. blue, 7 oz. each dk. blue and red; tapestry needle; I crochet hook or size needed to obtain gauge.

Gauge: 3 dc = 1"; 3 dc rows = 2". Each Motif is 2½" square.

Skill Level: ★★ Average

Basic Motif
(make 112 off-white, 64 med. blue, 52 dk. blue)

Rnd 1: Ch 4, sl st in first ch to form ring, ch 3, 2 dc in ring, ch 2, (3 dc in ring, ch 2) 3 times, join with sl st in top of ch-3 (12 dc, 4 ch sps).

Rnd 2: Ch 3, dc in each st around with (2 dc, ch 2, 2 dc) in each corner ch sp, join, fasten off (7 dc on each side between corner ch sps).

Half Motif
(make 32 med. blue/red, 12 off-white/dk. blue, 8 dk. blue/red)

Note: *When changing colors (see page 159), always drop yarn to wrong side of work. Use a separate skein of yarn for each color section.* **Do not** *carry yarn across from one section to another. Fasten off at end of each color section.*

Rnd 1: With blue, ch 4, sl st in first ch to form ring, ch 3, 2 dc in ring, ch 2, 3 dc in ring changing to red in last st made, ch 2, 3 dc in ring, ch 2, 3 dc in ring changing to blue in last st made, ch 2, join with sl st in top of ch-3 (12 dc, 4 ch sps).

Rnd 2: Ch 3, dc in each of next 2 sts, (2 dc, ch 2, 2 dc) in next ch sp, dc in each of next 3 sts, 2 dc in next sp changing to red in last st made, ch 2, 2 dc in same ch sp, dc in each of next 3 sts, (2 dc, ch 2, 2 dc) in next ch sp, dc in each of next 3 sts, 2 dc in next sp changing to blue in last st made, ch 2, 2 dc in same ch sp, join, fasten off (7 dc on each side between corner ch sps).

Quarter Motif
(make 32 med. blue/red, 8 dk. blue/red)

Rnd 1: With blue, ch 4, sl st in first ch to form ring, ch 3, 2 dc in ring, ch 2, 3 dc in ring, ch 2, 3 dc in ring changing to red in last st made, ch 2, 3 dc in ring changing to blue in last st made, ch 2, join with sl st in top of ch-3 (12 dc, 4 ch sps).

Rnd 2: Ch 3, dc in each of next 2 sts, *(2 dc, ch 2, 2 dc) in next ch sp, dc in each of next 3 sts; repeat from *, 2 dc in next sp changing to red in last st made, ch 2, 2 dc in same ch sp, dc in each of next 3 sts, 2 dc in next ch sp changing to blue in last st made, ch 2, 2 dc in same ch sp, join, fasten off (7 dc on each side between corner ch sps).

Holding Motifs wrong sides together, matching sts, with coordinating color, sew together through **back lps** according to Assembly Diagram.

Border

Rnd 1: Working around outer edge, in **back lps** only, skipping seams, join med. blue with sc in any st, sc in each st and in ch on each side of seam around with (sc in next ch, ch 1, sc in next ch) in each corner, join with sl st in first sc, fasten off (144 sc on each short end between corner ch sps, 180 on each long edge between corner ch sps).

Rnd 2: Join off-white with sc in corner ch sp before one short end, ch 2, sc in same sp, *[skip next st, sc in each st around to st before next corner ch sp, skip next st], (sc, ch 2, sc) in next corner ch sp; repeat from * 2 more times; repeat between [ ], join.

Rnd 3: Ch 3, (2 dc, ch 2, 2 dc) in next sp, *[dc in next st, ch 1, skip next 2 sts, dc in each of next 3 sts, (ch 1, skip next st, dc in each of next 3 sts) across] to 2 sts before next corner ch sp, ch 1, skip next st, dc in next st, (2 dc, ch 2, 2 dc) in next corner ch sp; repeat from * 2 more times; repeat between [ ], ch 1, skip last

Continued on page 72

Continued from page 70

st, join with sl st in top of ch-3 (111 dc and 36 ch-1 sps on each short end between corner ch sps, 138 dc and 45 ch-1 sps on each long edge between corner ch sps).

Rnd 4: Ch 4, skip next st, dc in next st, (2 dc, ch 2, 2 dc) in next ch sp, *dc in next st, ch 1, skip next st, (dc in next st, dc in next ch sp, dc in next st, ch 1, skip next st) across to st before next corner ch sp, dc in next st, (2 dc, ch 2, 2 dc) in next corner ch sp; repeat from * 2 more times, dc in next st, ch 1, skip next st, (dc in next st, dc in next ch sp, dc in next st, ch 1, skip next st) across to last st, dc in last st, dc in last ch sp, join (115 dc and 37 ch sps on each short end between corner ch sps, 142 dc and 46 ch sps on each long edge between corner ch sps).

Rnd 5: Ch 3, dc in next ch sp, dc in next st, ch 1, skip next st, dc in next st, (2 dc, ch 2, 2 dc) in next ch sp, *[dc in next st, ch 1, skip next 2 sts, (dc in next st, dc in next ch sp, dc in next st, ch 1, skip next st) across] to st before next corner ch sp, dc in next st, (2 dc, ch 2, 2 dc) in next corner ch sp; repeat from * 2 more times; repeat between [ ], join.

Rnd 6: Ch 1, sc in first st, ch 2, sc in next ch sp, ch 2, skip next st, (sc in next st, ch 2, sc in next ch sp, ch 2, skip next st) around, join with sl st in first sc, fasten off.

Assembly Diagram

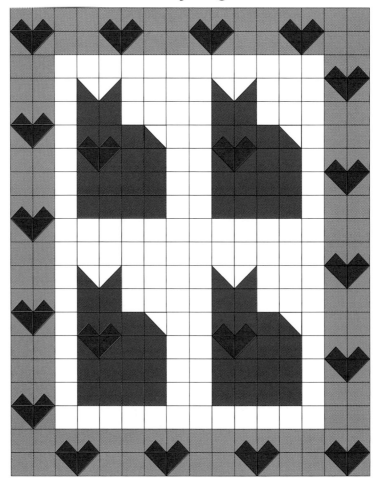

Americana Star

Continued from page 68

Rnd 2: Ch 2, hdc in each st around with 3 hdc in each center corner st, join, fasten off.

Block Graph

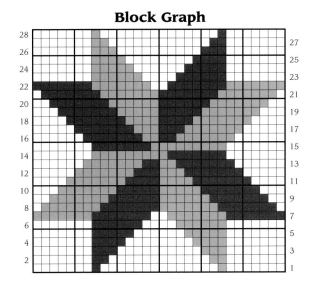

Each square equals 1 hdc.

■ = Red
■ = Blue
□ = White

Strip Graph

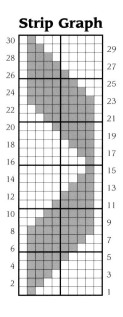

Flying Rainbows

Instuctions on page 67

□ = Navy blue
■ = Lt. green
□ = Med. green
■ = Dk. green
□ = Yellow
■ = Lt. peach
■ = Dk. peach
■ = Lt. orange
■ = Dk. orange
□ = Lt. blue
■ = Med. blue
■ = Turquoise
■ = Med. purple
■ = Dk. purple

Assembly Diagram

Tulips in Bloom

Designed by Maggie Weldon

Finished Size: 46" x 71".

Materials: Worsted-weight yarn — 48 oz. off-white, 16 oz. rose and 8 oz. green; tapestry needle; I crochet hook or size needed to obtain gauge.

Gauge: 7 sc = 2"; 4 sc rows = 1"; 2 dc rows = 1¼". Each Block is 9" x 14".

Skill Level: ★★ Average

Block
(make 25)

Notes: When changing colors (see page 159), always drop yarn to wrong side of work. Use a separate skein of yarn for each color section. **Do not** carry yarn across from one section to another. Fasten off at end of each color section.

Work odd-numbered rows on graph from right to left and even-numbered rows from left to right.

Each square on graph equals one sc.

Row 1: With off-white, ch 22, sc in 2nd ch from hook, sc in each ch across, turn (21 sc).

Row 2: Ch 1, sc in each st across, turn.

Row 3: For **row 3 of Block Graph** (see page 79), ch 1, sc in first 9 sts changing to green in last st made, sc in next st changing to off-white, sc in last 11 sts, turn.

Rows 4-44: Ch 1, sc in each st across changing colors according to Block Graph, turn. At end of last row, **do not** fasten off.

Rnd 45: Working around outer edge, ch 1, 3 sc in first st, sc in each st across to last st, 3 sc in last st; *working in ends of rows, skip first row, sc in next 7 rows, skip next row, (sc in next 6 rows, skip next row) across* to next corner; working in starting ch on opposite side of row 1, 3 sc in first ch, sc in each ch across to last ch, 3 sc in last ch; repeat between **, join with sl st in first sc, fasten off (21 sc across each short end between center corner sts, 39 sc across each long edge between center corner sts).

Note: For **cluster (cl),** yo, insert hook in next st, yo, draw lp through, yo, draw through 2 lps on hook, yo, insert hook in same st, yo, draw lp through, yo, draw through 2 lps on hook, yo, draw through all 3 lps on hook.

Rnd 46: Join rose with sl st in any center corner st, ch 3, yo, insert hook in same st, yo, draw lp through, yo, draw through 2 lps on hook, yo, draw through both lps on hook, ch 3, cl in same st, ch 1, skip next st, *[(cl in next st, ch 1, skip next st) across] to next center corner st, (cl, ch 3, cl) in next st; repeat from * 2 more times; repeat between [ ], join with sl st in top of ch-3, fasten off (11 ch sps on each short end between corner ch sps, 20 ch sps on each long edge between corner ch sps).

Rnd 47: Join off-white with sl st in any corner ch sp, ch 3, (2 dc, ch 2, 3 dc) in same sp, 2 dc in each ch-1 sp around with (3 dc, ch 2, 3 dc) in each corner ch sp, join, fasten off.

Holding Blocks wrong sides together, matching sts, with off-white, sew together through **back lps** in 5 rows of 5 Blocks each as shown in photo.

Tulip
(make 25)

Row 1: With rose, ch 4, 2 sc in 2nd ch from hook, sc in next ch, 2 sc in last ch, turn (5 sc).

Row 2: (Ch 2, sc) in first st, sc in each of next 3 sts, (sc, hdc) in last st, turn (7 sts).

Row 3: (Ch 2, sc) in first st, sc in next 5 sts, (sc, hdc) in last st, turn (9).

Rows 4-7: Ch 1, sc in each st across, turn.

Note: For **picot,** ch 3, sl st in 3rd ch from hook.

Row 8: Ch 5, sl st in 3rd ch from hook, dc in same st, sc in next st, *sl st in next st, ch 1, (dc, picot, dc) in next st, ch 1; repeat from *, sl st in next st, sc in next st, (2 dc, picot) in last st, **do not** turn.

Row 9: Working around bottom half of Tulip, sl st in end of each row and in each ch across to first st of last row, fasten off leaving long end for sewing.

Continued on page 79

Shining Stars

Designed by Carol Smith

Finished Size: 60" x 64".

Materials: Worsted-weight yarn — 24 oz. each turquoise and purple, 16 oz. each fuchsia and variegated; tapestry needle; I crochet hook or size needed to obtain gauge.

Gauge: 3 sts = 1"; 3 dc rows = 2". Each Star Motif is 20" across from side to side and 23" across from point to point. Each Half-Star Motif is 22" across long edge.

Skill Level: ★★ Average

Star Motif
(make 8)

Note: For **dc front post (fp)**, *yo, insert hook from front to back around post of next st (see page 159), yo, draw lp through, (yo, draw through 2 lps on hook) 2 times.*

Rnd 1: With fuchsia, ch 5, sl st in first ch to form ring, ch 3, 2 dc in ring, ch 1, (3 dc in ring, ch 1) 5 times, join with sl st in top of ch-3 (18 dc, 6 ch sps).

Rnd 2: Ch 3, *[fp around next st, dc in next st, (dc, ch 1, dc) in next ch sp], dc in next st; repeat from * 4 more times; repeat between [ ], join (30 sts, 6 ch sps).

Rnd 3: Ch 3, *[fp around next fp, dc in each of next 2 sts, (dc, ch 1, dc) in next ch sp], dc in each of next 2 sts; repeat from * 4 more times; repeat between [ ], dc in last st, join (42 sts, 6 ch sps).

Rnd 4: Ch 3, *[fp around next fp, dc in next st, fp around next st, dc in next st, (dc, ch 1, dc) in next ch sp, dc in next st, fp around next st], dc in next st; repeat from * 4 more times; repeat between [ ], join (54 sts, 6 ch sps).

Rnd 5: Ch 3, *[fp around next fp, dc in next st, fp around next fp, dc in each of next 2 sts, (dc, ch 1, dc) in next ch sp, dc in each of next 2 sts, fp around next st], dc in next st; repeat from * 4 more times; repeat between [ ], join, fasten off (66 sts, 6 ch sps).

Row 6: Working this row in **back lps** only, for **first point,** join variegated with sl st in any ch sp, ch 2, dc in each st across to last st before next ch sp, dc last st and next ch sp tog leaving remaining sts and ch sps unworked, turn (11 dc). Ch-2 at beginning of row is not used or counted as a st.

Rows 7-10: Ch 2, dc in each st across to last 2 sts, dc last 2 sts tog, turn, ending with 3 dc in last row.

Row 11: Ch 3, dc last 2 sts tog, turn, fasten off.

Row 6: Working this row in **back lps** only, for **next point,** join variegated with sl st in same ch sp as last point worked in on rnd 5, ch 2, dc in each st across to last st before next ch sp, dc last st and next ch sp tog leaving remaining sts and ch sps unworked, turn (13 dc).

Rows 7-10: Ch 2, dc in each st across to last 2 sts, dc last 2 sts tog, turn, ending with 3 dc in last row.

Row 11: Ch 2, dc last 2 sts tog, turn, fasten off.

Repeat next point 4 more times for a total of 6 points.

Note: For **treble cluster decrease (cl),** *yo 2 times, insert hook in end of next row, yo, draw lp through, (yo, draw through 2 lps on hook) 2 times, yo 2 times, insert hook in end of same row, yo, draw lp through, (yo, draw through 2 lps on hook) 2 times*; working over dc into ch sp of rnd 5, yo 3 times, insert hook in next sp, yo, draw lp through, (yo, draw through 2 lps on hook) 3 times; working in ends of rows on next point; repeat between **, yo, draw through all 6 lps on hook.*

Rnd 12: Working in ends of rows around outer edge, with right side facing you, join turquoise with sl st in dc of any point on row 11, ch 3, 4 dc in same st, (*2 dc in each of next 5 rows, cl, 2 dc in each of next 5 rows*, 5 dc in next dc on row 11) 5 times; repeat between **, join (150 dc, 6 cls).

Rnd 13: Ch 3, dc in next st, (*5 dc in next st, dc in next 11 sts, tr next 3 sts tog*, dc in

Continued from page 77

next 11 sts) 5 times; repeat between **, dc in last 9 sts, join (162 dc, 6 tr).

Rnd 14: Ch 2, (*sc in each of next 3 sts, 3 sc in next st, sc in each of next 3 sts, hdc in each of next 3 sts, dc in each of next 3 sts, tr in each of next 3 sts, tr next 3 sts tog, tr in each of next 3 sts, dc in each of next 3 sts*, hdc in each of next 3 sts) 5 times; repeat between **, hdc in each of last 2 sts, join with sl st in top of ch-2 (168 sts).

Rnd 15: Ch 2, hdc in next 4 sts, (*3 hdc in next st, hdc in next 8 sts, dc in next 11 sts*, hdc in next 8 sts) 5 times; repeat between **, hdc in each of last 3 sts, join, fasten off (180).

Rnd 16: Join turquoise with sl st in center st of 3-hdc group on any point, ch 3, 4 dc in same st, (*dc in each st across to center st of next 3-hdc group*, 5 dc in next st) 5 times; repeat between **, join with sl st in top of ch-3, fasten off (204 dc).

Half–Star Motif
(make 2)

Row 1: With fuchsia, ch 5, sl st in first ch to form ring, ch 3, 2 dc in ring, (ch 1, 3 dc in ring) 3 times, turn (12 dc, 3 ch sps).

Row 2: Ch 3, bp around next st, dc in next st, *(dc, ch 1, dc) in next ch sp, dc in next st, bp around next st, dc in next st; repeat from * across, turn (18 sts, 3 ch sps).

Row 3: Ch 3, fp around next st, *dc in each of next 2 sts, (dc, ch 1, dc) in next ch sp, dc in each of next 2 sts, fp around next st; repeat from * 2 more times, dc in last st, turn (24 sts, 3 ch sps).

Row 4: Ch 3, (bp around next st, dc in next st) 2 times, *(dc, ch 1, dc) in next ch sp, dc in next st, (bp around next st, dc in next st) 3 times; repeat from *, (dc, ch 1, dc) in next ch sp, dc in next st, (bp around next st, dc in next st) 2 times, turn (30 sts, 3 ch sps).

Row 5: Ch 3, fp around next st, dc in next st, fp around next st, dc in each of next 2 sts, (dc, ch 1, dc) in next ch sp, *dc in each of next 2 sts, (fp around next st, dc in next st) 2 times, fp around next st, dc in each of

next 2 sts, (dc, ch 1, dc) in next ch sp; repeat from *, dc in each of next 2 sts, (fp around next st, dc in next st) 2 times, **do not** turn, fasten off. (36 sts, 3 ch sps).

Row 6: Working this row in **back lps** only, for **first point,** join variegated with sl st in first st, ch 3, dc in each st across to st before next ch sp, dc next st and next ch sp tog leaving remaining sts and ch sps unworked, turn (7 dc).

Row 7: Ch 2, dc in each st across, turn (6).

Row 8: Ch 3, dc in each st across to last 2 sts, dc last 2 sts tog, turn (5).

Rows 9-10: Repeat rows 7 and 8 (4, 3).

Row 11: Ch 3, dc last 2 sts tog, turn, fasten off.

Row 6: Working this row in **back lps** only, for **next point,** join variegated with sl st in same ch sp as last point worked in on rnd 5, ch 2, dc in each st across to last st before next ch sp, dc last st and next ch sp tog leaving remaining sts and ch sps unworked, turn (11 dc).

Rows 7-10: Ch 2, dc in each st across to last 2 sts, dc last 2 sts tog, turn.

Row 11: Ch 2, dc last 2 sts tog, turn, fasten off.

Repeat next point for a total of 3 points.

Row 6: Working this row in **back lps** only, for **last point,** join variegated with sl st in same ch sp as last point worked in on rnd 5, ch 2, dc in each st across, turn (7 dc).

Row 7: Ch 3, dc in each st across to last 2 sts, dc last 2 sts tog, turn (6).

Row 8: Ch 2, dc in each st across, turn (5).

Rows 9-10: Repeat rows 7 and 8 (4, 3).

Row 11: Ch 3, dc last 2 sts tog, turn, fasten off.

Rnd 12: Working in sts and ends of rows around outer edge, with right side facing you, join turquoise with sl st in dc on row 11 of first point, ch 3, (dc, ch 1, 2 dc) in same st, *2 dc in ends of next 5 rows, cl, 2 dc in each of next 5 rows on next point, (2 dc, ch 1, 2 dc) in next dc on row 11; repeat from * 2 more times, 2 dc in each row across with dc in starting ring on row 1, join with sl st in top of ch-3 (121 dc, 4 ch sps, 3 cls).

Rnd 13: Ch 3, dc in next st, (2 dc, ch 1, 2 dc) in next ch sp, *[dc in next 11 sts, tr next 3 sts tog, dc in next 11 sts], 5 dc in next ch sp; repeat from *; repeat between [ ], (2 dc, ch 1, 2 dc) in next ch sp, dc in last 47 sts, join (136 sts, 2 ch sps).

Rnd 14: Ch 1, sc in first 4 sts, 3 sc in next ch sp, (*sc in each of next 3 sts, hdc in each of next 3 sts, dc in each of next 3 sts, tr in each of next 3 sts, tr next 3 sts tog, tr in each of next 3 sts, dc in each of next 3 sts, hdc in each of next 3 sts, sc in each of next 3 sts*, 3 sc in next st) 2 times; repeat between **, 3 sc in next ch sp, sc in last 49 sts, join with sl st in first sc (140 sts).

Rnd 15: Ch 1, sc in each of first 5 sts, (3 sc in next st, hdc in next 8 sts, dc in next 11 sts, hdc in next 8 sts) 3 times, 3 sc in next st, sc in last 50 sts, join, fasten off (148).

Rnd 16: Join purple with sl st in center st of 3-sc group on first point, ch 3, 4 dc in same st, (dc in each st across to center st of next 3-sc group, 5 dc in next st) 3 times, dc in each st across, join with sl st in top of ch-3, fasten off.

Holding Motifs wrong sides together, matching sts, with turquoise, sew together through **back lps** according to Assembly Diagram.

Border

Working around entire outer edge, join purple with sl st in any st, ch 3, evenly sp dc around with 5 dc in center st of each 5-dc group and dc in each seam increasing as needed for Afghan to lay flat, join with sl st in top of ch-3, fasten off.

Assembly Diagram

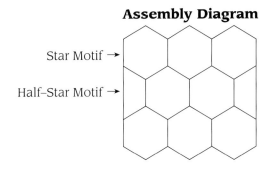

Star Motif →

Half–Star Motif →

Tulips in Bloom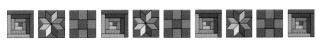

Continued from page 74

Sew one Tulip over rows 30-42 above stem on each Block.

Border

Working around entire outer edge, skipping seams, join off-white with sl st in any st, ch 3, dc in each st and in ch sps on each side of seams around with (2 dc, ch 2, 2 dc) in each corner ch sp, join with sl st in top of ch-3, fasten off.

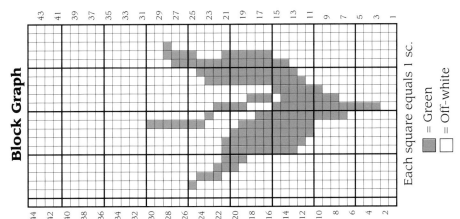

Block Graph

Each square equals 1 sc.

■ = Green   □ = Off-white

Hexagon Floral

Designed by Katherine Eng

Finished Size: 43" x 65½".

Materials: Worsted-weight yarn — 13 oz. each off-white and med. blue, 9 oz. green, 8 oz. each red and dk. blue; tapestry needle; G crochet hook or size needed to obtain gauge.

Gauge: Rnds 1-5 = 3¾" x 4¼" across. Each Motif is 6¼" across.

Skill Level: ★★ Average

Motif A
(make 25)

Note: For **dc cluster (cl),** (yo, insert hook in ring, yo, draw lp through, yo, draw through 2 lps on hook) 3 times, yo, draw through all 4 lps on hook.

Rnd 1: With off-white, ch 4, sl st in first ch to form ring, ch 3, (yo, insert hook in ring, yo, draw lp through, yo, draw through 2 lps on hook) 2 times, yo, draw through all 3 lps on hook, ch 2, (cl in ring, ch 2) 5 times, join with sl st in top of ch-3, fasten off (6 cls, 6 ch sps).

Rnd 2: Join med. blue with sc in any ch sp, 2 sc in same sp, ch 1, (3 sc in next ch sp, ch 1) around, join with sl st in first sc (18 sc, 6 ch sps).

Rnd 3: Ch 1, sc in each of first 3 sts, (sc, ch 2, sc) in next ch sp, *sc in each of next 3 sts, (sc, ch 2, sc) in next ch sp; repeat from * around, join, **turn** (30 sc, 6 ch sps).

Rnd 4: Ch 1, sc in first st, ch 1, skip next st, *[(sc, ch 2, sc) in next ch sp, ch 1, skip next st, (sc in next st, ch 1, skip next st)] 2 times; repeat from * 4 more times; repeat between [ ], join, **turn,** fasten off (24 ch sps).

Note: For **popcorn (pc),** 4 dc in next ch sp, drop lp from hook, insert hook in first st of 4-dc group, pick up dropped lp, draw through st.

Rnd 5: Join green with sc in any ch-2 sp, ch 2, sc in same sp, *[ch 1, hdc in next ch sp, ch 1, pc, ch 1, hdc in next ch sp, ch 1],

(sc, ch 2, sc) in next ch sp; repeat from * 4 more times; repeat between [ ], join, **turn** (30 ch sps).

Rnd 6: Sl st in first ch sp, ch 1, sc in same sp, ch 1, (sc in next ch sp, ch 1) 3 times, *[(sc, ch 2, sc) in next ch sp, ch 1], (sc in next ch sp, ch 1) 4 times; repeat from * 4 more times; repeat between [ ], join, **turn** (36 ch sps, 36 sc).

Rnd 7: Ch 1, sc in each st and in each ch-1 sp around with (sc, ch 2, sc) in each corner ch-2 sp, join, **do not** turn, fasten off.

Rnd 8: Join off-white with sc in any ch-2 sp, ch 1, sc in same sp, *[ch 1, skip next st, (sc in next st, ch 1, skip next st) 6 times], (sc, ch 1, sc) in next ch sp; repeat from * 4 more times; repeat between [ ], join, fasten off.

Motif B
(make 21)

Rnd 1: With off-white, ch 4, sl st in first ch to form ring, ch 3, (yo, insert hook in ring, yo, draw lp through, yo, draw through 2 lps on hook) 2 times, yo, draw through all 3 lps on hook, ch 2, (cl in ring, ch 2) 5 times, join with sl st in top of ch-3, fasten off (6 cls, 6 ch sps).

Rnd 2: Join med. blue with sc in any ch sp, 2 sc in same sp, ch 1, (3 sc in next ch sp, ch 1) around, join with sl st in first sc (18 sc, 6 ch sps).

Rnd 3: Ch 1, sc in each of first 3 sts, (sc, ch 2, sc) in next ch sp, *sc in each of next 3 sts, (sc, ch 2, sc) in next ch sp; repeat from * around, join, **turn** (30 sc, 6 ch sps).

Rnd 4: Ch 1, sc in first st, ch 1, skip next st, *[(sc, ch 2, sc) in next ch sp, ch 1, skip next st, (sc in next st, ch 1, skip next st)] 2 times; repeat from * 4 more times; repeat between [ ], join, **turn,** fasten off (24 ch sps).

Rnd 5: Join red with sc in any ch-2 sp,

Hexagon Floral

Continued from page 81

ch 2, sc in same sp, *[ch 1, hdc in next ch sp, ch 1, pc, ch 1, hdc in next ch sp, ch 1], (sc, ch 2, sc) in next ch sp; repeat from * 4 more times; repeat between [ ], join, **turn** (30 ch sps).

Rnd 6: Sl st in first ch sp, ch 1, sc in same sp, ch 1, (sc in next ch sp, ch 1) 3 times, *[(sc, ch 2, sc) in next ch sp, ch 1], (sc in next ch sp, ch 1) 4 times; repeat from * 4 more times; repeat between [ ], join, **turn** (36 ch sps, 36 sc).

Rnd 7: Ch 1, sc in each st and in each ch-1 sp around with (sc, ch 2, sc) in each corner ch-2 sp, join, **do not** turn, fasten off.

Rnd 8: Join off-white with sc in any ch-2 sp, ch 1, sc in same sp, *[ch 1, skip next st, (sc in next st, ch 1, skip next st) 6 times], (sc, ch 1, sc) in next ch sp; repeat from * 4 more times; repeat between [ ], join, fasten off.

Motif C
(make 21)

Rnd 1: With off-white, ch 4, sl st in first ch to form ring, ch 3, (yo, insert hook in ring, yo, draw lp through, yo, draw through 2 lps on hook) 2 times, yo, draw through all 3 lps on hook, ch 2, (cl in ring, ch 2) 5 times, join with sl st in top of ch-3, fasten off (6 cls, 6 ch sps).

Rnd 2: Join med. blue with sc in any ch sp, 2 sc in same sp, ch 1, (3 sc in next ch sp, ch 1) around, join with sl st in first sc (18 sc, 6 ch sps).

Rnd 3: Ch 1, sc in each of first 3 sts, (sc, ch 2, sc) in next ch sp, *sc in each of next 3 sts, (sc, ch 2, sc) in next ch sp; repeat from * around, join, **turn** (30 sc, 6 ch sps).

Rnd 4: Ch 1, sc in first st, ch 1, skip next st, *[(sc, ch 2, sc) in next ch sp, ch 1, skip next st, (sc in next st, ch 1, skip next st)] 2 times; repeat from * 4 more times; repeat between [ ], join, **turn,** fasten off (24 ch sps).

Rnd 5: Join dk. blue with sc in any ch-2 sp, ch 2, sc in same sp, *[ch 1, hdc in next

ch sp, ch 1, pc, ch 1, hdc in next ch sp, ch 1], (sc, ch 2, sc) in next ch sp; repeat from * 4 more times; repeat between [ ], join, **turn** (30 ch sps).

Rnd 6: Sl st in first ch sp, ch 1, sc in same sp, ch 1, (sc in next ch sp, ch 1) 3 times, *[(sc, ch 2, sc) in next ch sp, ch 1], (sc in next ch sp, ch 1) 4 times; repeat from * 4 more times; repeat between [ ], join, **turn** (36 ch sps, 36 sc).

Rnd 7: Ch 1, sc in each st and in each ch-1 sp around with (sc, ch 2, sc) in each corner ch-2 sp, join, **do not** turn, fasten off.

Rnd 8: Join off-white with sc in any ch-2 sp, ch 1, sc in same sp, *[ch 1, skip next st, (sc in next st, ch 1, skip next st) 6 times], (sc, ch 1, sc) in next ch sp; repeat from * 4 more times; repeat between [ ], join, fasten off.

Holding Motifs wrong sides together, matching sts, with off-white, sew together through **back lps** according to Assembly Diagram.

Border

Rnd 1: Working around entire outer edge, skipping seams, join off-white with sc in corner ch sp before one short end according to diagram (see page 72), ch 1, sc in same sp, *ch 1, (sc in next ch sp, ch 1) 7 times; for **peak,** (sc, ch 1, sc) in next ch sp, •ch 1, (sc in next ch sp, ch 1) 25 times, (sc, ch 1, sc) in next ch sp; repeat from * 2 more times, [ch 1, (sc in next ch sp, ch 1) 7 times, (sc, ch 1, sc) in next ch sp]; repeat between [ ], ◊ch 1, (sc in next ch sp, ch 1) 16 times, (sc, ch 1, sc) in next ch sp◊; repeat between ◊◊ 8 more times•; repeat between [ ] 2 times; repeat between ••, ch 1, (sc in next ch sp, ch 1) 7 times, join with sl st in first sc, **turn** (116 ch sps on each short end between corner ch sps, 179 ch sps on each long edge between corner ch sps).

Rnd 2: Ch 1, sc in first ch sp, ch 1, *(sc in next ch sp, ch 1) across to next peak, (sc, ch 1, sc) in next ch sp of peak, ch 1; repeat from * around, join, **turn,** fasten off (123 ch sps on each short end between corner ch sps, 190 ch sps on each long edge between corner ch sps).

Rnd 3: Join med. blue with sc in first corner ch sp, ch 2, sc in same sp, ◆*ch 2, skip next ch sp, (sc in next ch sp, ch 2, skip next ch sp) 4 times, (sc, ch 2, sc) in next ch sp, (ch 2, skip next ch sp, sc in next ch sp) 4 times, ch 1, skip next st, sc in next st, ch 1, skip next st, sc in next ch sp, (ch 2, skip next ch sp, sc in next ch sp) 3 times, ch 1, skip next st, sc in next st, ch 1, skip next st, sc in next ch sp, ch 2, skip next ch sp, (sc in next ch sp, ch 2, skip next ch sp) 3 times, (sc, ch 2, sc) in next ch sp; repeat from * 2 more times, [ch 2, skip next ch sp, (sc in next ch sp, ch 2, skip next ch sp) 4 times, (sc, ch 2, sc) in next ch sp]; repeat between [ ], ◊(ch 2, skip next ch sp, sc in next ch sp) 4 times, ch 1, skip next st, sc in next st, ch 1, skip next st, (sc in next ch sp, ch 2, skip next ch sp) 4 times, (sc, ch 2, sc) in next ch sp; repeat from ◊ 8 more times◆; repeat between [ ]; repeat between ◆◆, ch 2, skip next ch sp, (sc in next ch sp, ch 2, skip next ch sp) 4 times, join, **do not** turn.

Note: *For **shell,** (2 dc, ch 2, 2 dc) in next ch sp.*

Rnd 4: Sl st in next ch sp, ch 3, (dc, ch 2, 2 dc) in same sp, ◊(sc in next ch sp, shell in next ch sp) 5 times, *skip next ch sp, sc in next sc, skip next ch sp, shell in next ch sp, sc in next ch sp, shell in next ch sp, skip next ch sp, sc in next sc, skip next ch sp, (shell in next ch sp, sc in next ch sp) 7 times, shell in next ch sp; repeat from * 2 more times, (sc in next ch sp, shell in next ch sp) 3 times, [skip next ch sp, sc in next sc, skip next ch sp, (shell in next ch sp, sc in next ch sp) 4 times, shell in next ch sp]; repeat between [ ] 8 more times◊, sc in next ch sp, shell in next ch sp; repeat between ◊◊, sc in last ch sp, join with sl st in top of ch-3.

Rnd 5: Sl st in next dc, sl st in next ch sp, ch 1, (sc, ch 2, sc) in same sp, *ch 2, sc in next sc, ch 2, (sc, ch 2, sc) in ch sp of next shell; repeat from * around to last sc, ch 2, sc in last sc, ch 2, join with sl st in first sc, fasten off. ✑

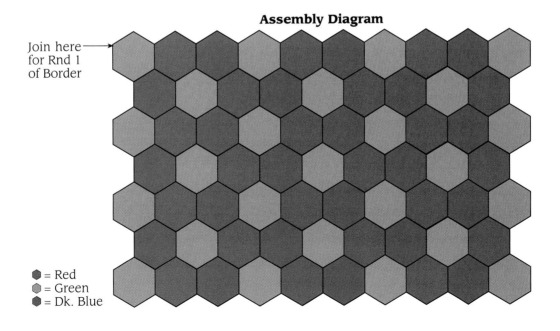

Assembly Diagram

Join here for Rnd 1 of Border

● = Red
● = Green
● = Dk. Blue

Legends

Rediscover the greatness of our dynamic American heritage among the rich colors and artistic lines of these spirited throws and blankets. From the shores of the founding Colonies across the rolling fruited plains to the vast Western sky, we have a legacy of freedom we should honor with each rising sun. Show your gratitude for those who paved the way with this stirring collection of hallmark designs.

Native Colors

Designed by Susie Spier Maxfield

Finished Size: 55" x 66" not including Fringe.

Materials: Worsted-weight yarn — 22 oz. aran fleck, 8 oz. each charcoal fleck, green fleck, navy fleck, tan fleck and maroon fleck; I hook or size needed to obtain gauge.

Gauge: 3 dc = 1; 3 dc rows = 2".

Skill Level: ★★ Average

Afghan

Notes: Each square on graph equals 2 dc.

*When changing colors (see page 159), always drop yarn to wrong side of work. Use a separate ball of yarn for each color section. **Do not** carry yarn across from one section to another. Fasten off colors at end of each color section.*

Beginning ch-3 is used and counted as first st of each row.

Work each row on graph from right to left, then repeat same row from left to right. Work center of row marked on graph only one time.

Row 1: With aran, ch 168, dc in 4th ch from hook, dc in each ch across, turn (166 dc).

Row 2: For **row 2 of graph,** ch 3, dc in next 17 sts changing to green in last st made, dc in each of next 2 sts changing to aran in last st made, (dc in next 30 sts changing to green in last st made, dc in each of next 2 sts changing to aran in last st made) 4 times, dc in last 18 sts, turn.

Rows 3-93: Ch 3, dc in each st across changing colors according to graph, turn. At end of last row, fasten off.

Row 94: Working in starting ch on opposite side of row 1, join aran with sl st in first st, ch 3, dc in each st across, turn.

Rows 95-96: Ch 3, dc in each st across, turn.

Rows 97-99: Ch 3, dc in each st across changing colors according to rows 91-93 on graph, turn. At end of last row, fasten off.

Fringe

For **each Fringe,** cut 3 strands yarn (see below for colors) each 16" long. Holding all strands together, fold in half, insert hook in st, draw fold through, draw all loose ends through fold, tighten. Trim ends.

Fringe in every other st across short ends of Afghan alternating color combinations of aran/maroon/navy and tan/charcoal/green.

Graph

☐ = Aran   ■ = Maroon   ▨ = Tan
■ = Navy   ▨ = Green   ▨ = Charcoal

Each square on graph equals 2 dc.
Center of row (work only once—do not repeat)

Twilight Trails

Designed by Tammy Hildebrand

Finished Size: 43" x 57".

Materials: Fuzzy bulky-weight yarn — 18 oz. green and 17 oz. green/orange/red variegated; tapestry needle; J hook or size needed to obtain gauge.

Gauge: Row 1 = 1½" wide; rows 1-9 of Strip = 7".

Skill Level: ★★ Average

Strip
(make 8)

Notes: For **cluster (cl)**, *ch 3, yo, insert hook in top of last dc made, yo, draw lp through, yo, draw through 2 lps on hook, (yo, insert hook in same st, yo, draw lp through, yo, draw through 2 lps on hook) 2 times, yo, draw through all 4 lps on hook.*

Ch-4 at beginning of each row counts as first dc and ch-1 sp.

Row 1: With variegated, ch 10, dc in 8th ch from hook, cl; working over last dc made, skip next ch, dc in next ch; working forward, ch 1, skip next ch, dc in last ch, turn (4 dc, 2 ch-1 sps, 1 cl).

Rows 2-65: Ch 4, skip next dc and next cl, dc in next dc, cl; working over last dc made, dc in skipped dc, ch 1, dc in last st, turn.

Row 66: Ch 4, skip next dc and next cl, dc in next dc, ch 1; working over last dc made, dc in skipped dc, ch 1, dc in last st, fasten off. Push all cl to right side of work.

Rnd 67: With right side facing you, working across sts of last row, join green with sl st in first st, ch 3, (dc, ch 3, 2 dc) in same st, skip next ch-1 sp, 2 dc in next ch-1 sp, skip next ch-1 sp, (2 dc, ch 3, 2 dc) in last st; working in end of rows, 2 dc in top of each row across; working in starting ch on opposite side of row 1, (2 dc, ch 3, 2 dc) in first ch, skip next ch, 2 dc in ch between next 2 dc, skip next ch, (2 dc, ch 3, 2 dc) in last ch; working in end of rows, 2 dc in top of each row across, join with sl st in top of ch-3, fas-

ten off (3 2-dc groups between corner ch sps on each short end, 67 2-dc groups between corner ch sps on each long edge).

Rnd 68: Join variegated with sl st in first corner ch sp, ch 2, (hdc, ch 2, 2 hdc) in same sp; *working in sps between 2-dc groups, 2 hdc in each of next 2 sps, (2 hdc, ch 2, 2 hdc) in next corner ch sp; working in sps between 2-dc groups, 2 hdc in each sp across to next corner ch sp*, (2 hdc, ch 2, 2 hdc) in next ch sp; repeat between **, join with sl st in top of ch-2, fasten off (4 2-hdc groups between corner ch sps on each short end, 68 2-hdc groups between corner ch sps on each long edge).

Rnd 69: Join green with sc in first corner ch sp, ch 3, sc in same sp, *ch 3; working in sps between 2-hdc groups, (sc in next sp, ch 3) 3 times, (sc, ch 3, sc) in next corner ch sp, ch 3; working in sps between 2-hdc groups, (sc in next sp, ch 3) across* to next corner ch sp, (sc, ch 3, sc) in next ch sp; repeat between **, join with sl st in first sc, **do not** fasten off (4 ch sps between corner ch sps on each short end, 68 ch sps between corner ch sps on each long edge).

Rnd 70: Sl st in first ch sp, ch 2, (hdc, ch 2, 2 hdc) in same sp, 2 hdc in each ch sp across to next corner ch sp, *(2 hdc, ch 2, 2 hdc) in next ch sp, 2 hdc in each ch sp across to next corner ch sp; repeat from * 2 more times, join with sl st in top of ch-2, fasten off (6 2-hdc groups between corner ch sps across each short end, 70 2-hdc groups between corner ch sps across each long edge).

Holding Strips wrong sides together, matching sts, with green, sew long edges together through **back lps.**

Border

Rnd 1: Working around entire outer edge, with right side facing you, join green

Continued on page 93

Thunderbird

Designed by Rhonda Simpson

Finished Size: 51" x 61".

Materials: Worsted-weight yarn —16 oz. off-white, 14 oz. lt. coral rose, 8 oz. spruce and 6 oz. variegated; K hook or size needed to obtain gauge.

Gauge: 5 sc = 2"; 13 sc rows = 4".

Skill Level: ★★ Average

Center

Notes: *When changing colors (see page 159), always drop yarn to wrong side of work. Use a separate ball of yarn for each color section.* **Do not** *carry yarn across from one section to another. Fasten off colors at end of each color section.*

Work each row on graph from right to left, then repeat same row from left to right.

Each square on graph equals one sc.

Row 1: With off-white, ch 101, sc in 2nd ch from hook, sc in each ch across, turn (100 sc).

Rows 2-14: Ch 1, sc in each st across, turn.

Row 15: For **row 15 of Center Graph A** (see page 92), ch 1, sc in first 49 sts changing to coral rose in last st made, sc in each of next 2 sts changing to off-white in last st made, sc in each st across, turn.

Rows 16-80: Ch 1, sc in each st across changing colors according to Center Graph A, turn.

Rows 81-145: Ch 1, sc in each st across changing colors according to Center Graph B (see page 93), turn.

Rows 146-159: With off-white, ch 1, sc in each st across, turn.

Rnd 160: For **edging,** working in rnds, ch 1, 3 sc in first st, sc in each st across to last st, 3 sc in last st; *working in end of rows, skip first row, sc in next 4 rows, (skip next row, sc in next 5 rows, skip next row, sc in next 4 rows) across*; working in starting ch on opposite side of row 1, 3 sc in first ch, sc in each ch across to last ch, 3 sc in

last ch; repeat between **, join with sl st in first sc, fasten off.

End Border

Row 1: Working in rows across one short end of Center, join coral rose with sc in 3rd sc of first 3-sc corner, sc in each st across to next 3-sc corner, sc in next st leaving remaining sts unworked, turn (100 sc).

Notes: *Begin each row on graph at right-hand edge.*

Each square on graph equals one sc.

Row 2: Ch 1, sc in each st across, turn.

Rows 3-17: Changing colors according to Border Graph (see page 93), ch 1, sc in each st across to line B, repeat between line A and line B one time, sc in last 5 sts, turn. At end of last row, fasten off.

Repeat on opposite short end of Center.

Side Border

Row 1: Working across one long side of Center, join coral rose with sc in 3rd st of first 3-sc corner, sc in each st across to next 3-sc corner, sc in next st leaving remaining sts unworked, turn (132 sc).

Rows 2-17: Changing colors according to Border Graph, ch 1, sc in each st across to line B, (repeat between line A and line B) 2 times, sc in last 5 sts, turn. At end of last row, fasten off.

Repeat on opposite long side of Center. At end of last row, **do not** fasten off.

For **Border edging,** working around entire outer edge of End Borders and Side Borders, ch 1, 3 sc in first st, sc in each st across to last st, 3 sc in last st; *[working in end of rows, skip first row, sc in next 16 rows, sc in center st of next 3-sc corner on Center, sc in next 16 rows, skip next row]; working in sts across next Border, 3 sc in first st, sc in each st across to last st, 3 sc in last st; repeat from * 2 more times; repeat between [ ], join with sl st in first sc, fasten off.

Continued on page 92

Thunderbird

Continued from page 90

Border Squares

Row 1: Working in sp between one End Border and one Side Border, join spruce with sc in 3rd st of first 3-sc corner, sc in next 4 sts, (sc next 2 sts tog, sc in next 4 sts) 2 times, skip next st, sc in next 4 sts, (sc next 2 sts tog, sc in next 4 sts) 2 times, sc in next st leaving remaining sts unworked, turn (30 sc).

Row 2: Ch 1, sc in first 14 sts, skip next 2 sts, sc in last 14 sts, turn (28).

Row 3: Ch 1, sc in first 13 sts, skip next 2 sts, sc in last 13 sts, turn (26).

Row 4: Ch 1, sc in first 12 sts, skip next 2 sts, sc in last 12 sts, turn (24).

Row 5: Ch 1, sc in first 11 sts, skip next 2 sts, sc in last 11 sts, turn (22).

Row 6: Ch 1, sc in first 10 sts, skip next 2 sts, sc in last 10 sts, turn (20).

Row 7: Ch 1, sc in first 9 sts, skip next 2 sts, sc in last 9 sts, turn (18).

Row 8: Ch 1, sc in first 8 sts, skip next 2 sts, sc in last 8 sts, turn (16).

Row 9: Ch 1, sc in first 7 sts, skip next 2 sts, sc in last 7 sts, turn (14).

Row 10: Ch 1, sc in first 6 sts, skip next 2 sts, sc in last 6 sts, turn (12).

Row 11: Ch 1, sc in first 5 sts, skip next 2 sts, sc in last 5 sts, turn (10).

Row 12: Ch 1, sc in first 4 sts, skip next 2 sts, sc in last 4 sts, turn (8).

Row 13: Ch 1, sc in each of first 3 sts, skip next 2 sts, sc in each of last 3 sts, turn (6).

Row 14: Ch 1, sc in each of first 2 sts, skip next 2 sts, sc in each of last 2 sts, turn (4).

Row 15: Ch 1, sc in first st, skip next 2 sts, sc in last st, turn (2).

Row 16: Ch 1, sc next 2 sts tog, fasten off (1).

Repeat in remaining sps between End Borders and Side Borders ending with a total of 4 Border Squares. At end of last Border Square, **do not** fasten off.

For **edging,** working around entire outer edge of Afghan, ch 1, sc in each st around with 3 sc in each corner, join with sl st in first sc, fasten off.

☐ = Off-White
■ = Coral Rose
■ = Variegated
▨ = Spruce

Center Graph A

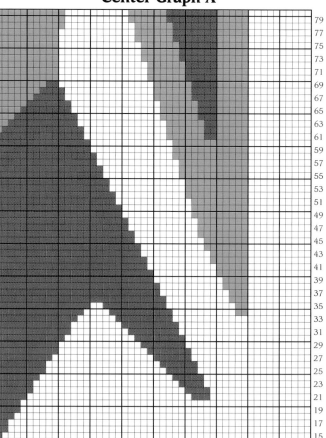

Each square on graph equals one sc.

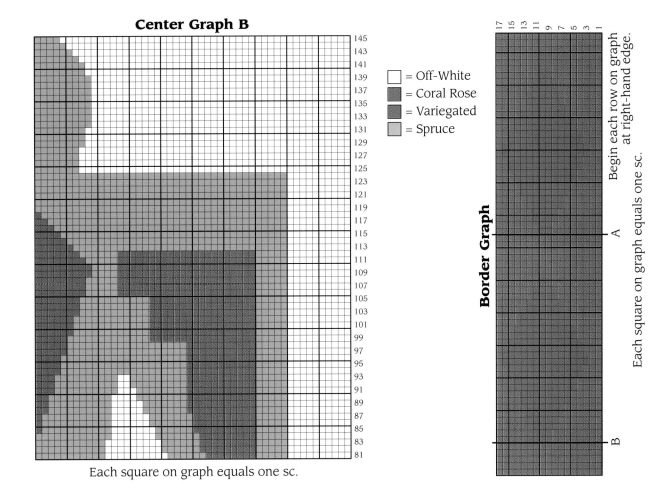

Center Graph B

145
143
141
139
137
135
133
131
129
127
125
123
121
119
117
115
113
111
109
107
105
103
101
99
97
95
93
91
89
87
85
83
81

☐ = Off-White
▨ = Coral Rose
▦ = Variegated
▨ = Spruce

Each square on graph equals one sc.

Border Graph

17 15 13 11 9 7 5 3 1

Begin each row on graph at right-hand edge.

A

B

Each square on graph equals one sc.

Twilight Trails

Continued from page 89

with sc in first corner ch sp before one short end, ch 3, sc in same sp, [ch 3; working in sps between 2-hdc groups, (sc in next sp, ch 3) 5 times, *hdc in next seam, ch 3, (sc in next sp, ch 3) 5 times; repeat from * across to next corner ch sp, (sc, ch 3, sc) in next ch sp, ch 3; working in sps between 2-hdc groups, (sc in next sp, ch 3) across] to next corner ch sp, (sc, ch 3, sc) in next ch sp; repeat between [ ], join with sl st in first sc.

Rnd 2: Sl st in first ch sp, ch 2, (hdc, ch 2, 2 hdc) in same sp, 2 hdc in each ch sp around with (2 hdc, ch 2, 2 hdc) in each corner ch sp, join with sl st in top of ch-2, fasten off.

Rnd 3: Join variegated with sl st in first corner ch sp, ch 2, (hdc, ch 2, 2 hdc) in same sp; working in sps between 2-hdc groups, 2 hdc in each sp around with (2 hdc, ch 2, 2 hdc) in each corner ch sp, join, fasten off. ✐

Cool Water

Designed by Maggie Weldon

Finished Size: 53" x 58" not including Fringe.

Materials: Fuzzy bulky-weight yarn —28 oz. each lilac and dusty gray, 21 oz. white; tapestry needle; J hook or size needed to obtain gauge.

Gauge: 3 dc = 1"; 5 dc rows = 3".

Skill Level: ★ Easy

Afghan

Row 1: With lilac, ch 114, dc in 4th ch from hook, dc in each ch across, turn (112 dc).

Row 2: Ch 3, dc in each st across, turn, fasten off.

Row 3: Join white with sl st in first st, ch 3, dc in each st across, turn, fasten off.

Row 4: Join dusty gray with sl st in first st, ch 3, dc in each st across, turn.

Row 5: Ch 3, dc in each st across, turn, fasten off.

Row 6: Join white with sl st in first st, ch 3, dc in each st across, turn, fasten off.

Row 7: Join lilac with sl st in first st, ch 3, dc in each st across, turn.

Row 8: Ch 3, dc in each st across, turn, fasten off.

Rows 9-98: Repeat rows 3-8 consecutively.

Woven Fringe

For **each Fringe,** beginning at bottom left-hand corner of Afghan, starting from right side of work and working under then over, weave 3 strands yarn held together (see below for colors) vertically through spaces between sts across to top left-hand corner leaving 6" at each end. Knot ends close to edge of Afghan.

Weaving through next spaces between sts, start next column of weaving from wrong side of work and weave over then under across Afghan.

Weave in color sequence of 4 lilac Fringe, 2 white Fringe, 4 dusty gray Fringe and 2 white Fringe across short ends of Afghan, ending with lilac. ✍

Country Meadows

Designed by Eleanor Albano-Miles

Finished Size: 49" x 59".

Materials: Worsted-weight yarn — 30 oz. mint/plum/rust variegated, 16 oz. each dk. mint and lt. mint; H hook or size needed to obtain gauge.

Gauge: 7 sts = 2"; 3 dc rows and 2 sc rows = 2".

Skill Level: ★★ Average

Strip
(make 7)

Row 1: With variegated, ch 182, tr in 6th ch from hook, (ch 1, skip next ch, tr in next ch) across, fasten off (90 tr, 89 ch sps).

Note: *For* **treble crochet front post (tr fp),** *yo 2 times, insert hook from front to back around post of next st (see page 159), yo, draw lp through, (yo, draw through 2 lps on hook) 3 times.*

Rnd 2: Working in rnds, join variegated with sl st in end of row 1, ch 3, 14 dc in end of same row, *tr fp around next st, (dc in next ch sp, tr fp around next st) 87 times*, 15 dc in opposite end of row 1; working in starting ch on opposite side of row 1, repeat between **, join with sl st in top of ch-3, **turn,** fasten off (380 sts).

Rnd 3: Join dk. mint with sc in first st, sc in each st around, join with sl st in first sc, **turn,** fasten off.

Rnd 4: Join lt. mint with sl st in first st, ch

3, *tr fp around corresponding st on rnd before last, (dc in next st on last rnd, tr fp around corresponding st on rnd before last) 15 times, (dc in next st on last rnd, tr fp around next fp on rnd before last, skip next st on last rnd) 87 times*, dc in next st; repeat between **, join with sl st in top of ch-3, **turn,** fasten off (412).

Rnd 5: With variegated, repeat rnd 3.

Rnd 6: Join dk. mint with sl st in first st, ch 3, tr fp around next fp on rnd before last, skip next st on last rnd, (dc in next st, tr fp around next fp on rnd before last, skip next st on last rnd) around, join with sl st in top of ch-3, **turn,** fasten off.

Rnd 7: With lt. mint, repeat rnd 3.

Rnd 8: With variegated, repeat rnd 6, **do not** fasten off.

Rnd 9: Ch 3, hdc in next st, ch 1, hdc in next st, *ch 1, skip next st, (hdc in next st, ch 1, skip next st) 86 times*, hdc in next st, (ch 1, hdc in next st) 32 times; repeat between **, (hdc in next st, ch 1) 30 times, join with sl st in 2nd ch of ch-3, fasten off.

To **join Strips,** holding 2 Strips right sides together, matching sts and working through both thicknesses, skipping center 23 ch sps on one end, join variegated with sl st in next ch sp, (ch 1, sl st in next ch sp) across to center 23 ch sps on opposite end, fasten off.

Repeat with remaining Strips. ✏

Indian Summer

Designed by Frances Hughes

Finished Size: 58" x 64".

Materials: Worsted-weight yarn — 33 oz. variegated, 14 oz. green, 10½ oz. each burgundy and rust, 4 oz. purple; H hook or size needed to obtain gauge.

Gauge: 7 sc = 2"; 7 sc rows = 2".

Skill Level: ★★ Average

Afghan

Row 1: For **center,** with green, ch 143, sc in 2nd ch from hook, sc in each ch across, turn (142 sc)

Rows 2-8: Ch 1, sc in each st across, turn. At end of last row, fasten off.

Row 9: Join variegated with sc in first st, sc in each st across, turn.

Rows 10-16: Repeat rows 2-8.

Row 17: With green, repeat row 9.

Rows 18-24: Repeat rows 2-8.

Row 25: With burgundy, repeat row 9.

Rows 26-50: Ch 1, sc in each st across, turn. At end of last row, fasten off.

Row 51: With green, repeat row 9.

Rows 52-58: Repeat rows 2-8.

Rows 59-124: Repeat rows 9-58 consecutively, ending with row 24.

Row 125: For **first section,** working in end of rows on one side of center (see Section Diagram on page 105), join rust with sc in last row, sc in each row across, turn (124).

Rows 126-138: Ch 1, sc in each st across, turn. At end of last row, fasten off.

Row 139: For **2nd section,** working in end of rows on other side of center, join rust with sc in first row, sc in each row across, turn (124).

Rows 140-152: Ch 1, sc in each st across, turn. At end of last row, fasten off.

Note: *When changing colors (see page 159), always drop yarn to wrong side of work. Use a separate skein or ball of yarn for each section.* **Do not** *Carry yarn across from one section to another. Fasten off colors at end of each color section.*

Row 153: For **3rd section,** working in end of rows on first and 2nd sections and in sts across row 124 of center, join purple with sc in first row, sc in next 13 rows changing to rust in last st made, sc in each st across row 124 changing to purple in last st made, sc in last 14 rows, turn.

Rows 154-166: Ch 1, sc in each st across changing colors according to established color pattern, turn. At end of last row, fasten off.

Rows 167-180: For **4th section,** working in end of rows on first and 2nd sections and in starting ch on opposite side of row 1 on center, repeat rows 153-166.

Row 181: For **5th section,** working in end of rows on 3rd and 4th sections and in sts across last row of first section, join variegated with sc in first row, sc in each row and in each st across, turn.

Rows 182-206: Ch 1, sc in each st across, turn. At end of last row, fasten off.

Rows 207-232: For **6th section,** working in end of rows on 3rd and 4th sections and in sts across last row of 2nd section, repeat rows 181-206.

Row 233: For **7th section,** working in end of rows on 5th and 6th sections and in sts across last row of 3rd section, join purple with sc in first row, sc in next 25 rows changing to variegated in last st made, sc in each st across changing to purple in last st made, sc in last 26 rows, turn.

Rows 234-258: Ch 1, sc in each st across changing colors according to established color pattern, turn. At end of last row, fasten off.

Rows 259-284: For **8th section,** working in end of rows on 5th and 6th sections and in sts across last row of 4th section, repeat rows 233-258.

Continued on page 105

Rustic Cabins

Designed by Eleanor Albano-Miles

Finished Size: 47" x 65½".

Materials: 4-ply bouclé yarn — 19 oz. each rust/plum/purple variegated (A) and teal/rust/blue variegated (B); worsted-weight yarn — 15 oz. each rust and teal; tapestry needle; H hook or size needed to obtain gauge.

Gauge: 7 sc = 2"; 4 sc rows = 1".

Skill Level: ★★ Average

Square A
(make 18)

Row 1: For **center,** with rust, ch 10, sc in 2nd ch from hook, sc in each ch across, turn (9 sc).

Rows 2-10: Ch 1, sc in each st across, turn. At end of last row, **do not** turn, fasten off.

Row 11: For **first section** (see Section Diagram on page 105), join variegated A with sl st in first st, ch 3, dc in next 7 sts, (2 dc, ch 2, 2 dc) in last st; working in end of rows, evenly space 8 dc across, turn (20 dc, 1 ch-2 sp).

Row 12: Ch 3, dc in next 9 sts, (2 dc, ch 2, 2 dc) in next ch-2 sp, dc in last 10 sts, turn, fasten off.

Row 13: For **2nd section,** join teal with sl st in end of row 12 on first section, ch 3, dc in same row, 2 dc in end of next row; working in starting ch on opposite side of row 1 on center, dc in next 8 chs, (2 dc, ch 2, 2 dc) in last ch; working in ends of rows across center, evenly space 8 dc across; working in ends of rows on opposite end of section 1, 2 dc in each of last 2 rows, turn (28 dc, 1 ch-2 sp).

Rows 14-15: Ch 3, dc in each st across to next ch-2 sp, (2 dc, ch 2, 2 dc) in next ch-2 sp, dc in each st across, turn, ending with 36 dc and 1 ch-2 sp in last row. At end of last row, **do not** turn, fasten off.

Row 16: For **3rd section,** working in ends of rows on 2nd section, join rust with sl st in row 15, ch 3, dc in same row, 2 dc in each of next 2 rows; working in sts across row 12 of first section, skip first st, dc in next 11 sts, (2 dc, ch 2, 2 dc) in next ch-2 sp, dc in next 11 sts; working in ends of rows on opposite end of 2nd section, 2 dc in each of next 3 rows, turn (38 dc, 1 ch-2 sp).

Row 17: Ch 3, dc in next 18 sts, (2 dc, ch 2, 2 dc) in next ch-2 sp, dc in last 19 sts, turn, fasten off (42 dc, 1 ch-2 sp).

Row 18: For **4th section,** working in ends of rows on 3rd section, join variegated B with sl st in row 17, ch 3, dc in same row, 2 dc in next row; working in sts across row 15 of 2nd section, dc in next 18 sts, (2 dc, ch 2, 2 dc) in next ch-2 sp, dc in next 18 sts; working in ends of rows on opposite end of 3rd section, 2 dc in each of last 2 rows, turn (48 dc, 1 ch-2 sp).

Row 19: Ch 3, dc in next 23 sts, (2 dc, ch 2, 2 dc) in next ch-2 sp, dc in last 24 sts, turn, fasten off (52 dc, 1 ch-2 sp).

Row 20: Working in sts across last row only, join teal with sl st in first st, ch 3, dc in next 25 sts, (2 dc, ch 2, 2 dc) in next ch-2 sp, dc in last 26 sts, fasten off.

Square B
(make 17)

Work same as Square A, reversing rust and teal and reversing variegated A and variegated B.

Matching colors, sew Squares A and B together according to Assembly Diagram (see page 105).

Border

Rnd 1: Working around entire outer edge, with right side facing you, join rust with sc in any corner ch-2 sp, (sc, ch 2, 2 sc) in same sp, sc in each st, sc in each ch sp on each side of seams and 2 sc in end of each row around with (2 sc, ch 2, 2 sc) in each corner ch sp, join with sl st in first sc, **turn.**

Continued on page 105

Square Dance

Designed by Katherine Eng

Finished Size: 47½" x 64½".

Materials: Worsted-weight yarn — 19 oz. med. brown, 16 oz. tan, 8 oz. rust and 6 oz. dk. brown; tapestry needle; G hook or size needed to obtain gauge.

Gauge: Rnds 1-4 of Square = 3¾" across. Each Square is 8½" square.

Skill Level: ★★ Average

Square
(make 35)

Rnd 1: With med. brown, ch 4, sl st in first ch to form ring, ch 1, 8 sc in ring, join with sl st in first sc (8 sc).

Note: For **puff st,** *yo, insert hook in next st, yo, draw up long lp, (yo, insert hook in same st, yo, draw up long lp) 3 times, yo, draw through all 9 lps on hook.*

Rnd 2: Ch 1, puff st in first st, ch 2, (puff st in next st, ch 2) around, join with sl st in first puff st (8 puff sts, 8 ch sps).

Rnd 3: Ch 1, sc in each puff st and 3 sc in each ch sp around, join with sl st in first sc, **turn** (32 sc).

Rnd 4: Ch 1, sc in each st around, join, **turn,** fasten off.

Rnd 5: Join tan with sc in first st, ch 2, sc in same st, sc in each of next 3 sts, *(sc, ch 2, sc) in next st, sc in each of next 3 sts; repeat from * around, join, **turn** (40 sc, 8 ch sps).

Rnd 6: Sl st in next st, ch 1, sc in same st, *[ch 2, skip next st, sc in next st, ch 1, skip next st, (sc, ch 2, sc) in next ch sp, ch 1, skip next st], sc in next st; repeat from * 6 more times; repeat between [ ], join, **turn** (16 ch-2 sps, 16 ch-1 sps).

Note: For **shell,** *3 dc in next st.*

Rnd 7: Sl st in first ch-1 sp, ch 1, sc in same sp, *[(sc, ch 2, sc) in next ch-2 sp, sc in next ch-1 sp, shell in next ch-2 sp], sc in next ch-1 sp; repeat from * 6 more times; repeat between [ ], join, **turn** (8 shells, 8 ch-2 sps).

Rnd 8: Sl st in each of next 2 sts, ch 1, sc in same st, ch 3, (sc, ch 2, sc) in next ch-2 sp, ch 3, *sc in center dc of next shell, ch 3, (sc, ch 2, sc) in next ch-2 sp, ch 3; repeat from * around, join, **turn** (24 sc, 16 ch-3 sps, 8 ch-2 sps).

Rnd 9: Ch 1, sc in each st, 3 sc in each ch-3 sp and 3 sc in each ch-2 sp around, join, **do not** turn, fasten off (96 sc).

Row 10: For **first triangle,** working in rows, join dk. brown with sl st in center st of any 3-sc point, ch 1, sc first 2 sts tog, sc in next 9 sts, sc next 2 sts tog leaving remaining sts unworked, turn (11 sc).

Rows 11-14: Ch 1, sc first 2 sts tog, sc in each st across to last 2 sts, sc last 2 sts tog, turn, ending with 3 sts in last row.

Row 15: Ch 1, insert hook in first st, yo, draw lp through, insert hook in next st, yo, draw lp through, yo, draw through all 3 lps on hook (first dec made), insert hook in same st, yo, draw lp through, insert hook in next st, yo, draw lp through, yo, draw through all 3 lps on hook (last dec made), turn (2 sc).

Row 16: Ch 2, skip first st, sc in last st, fasten off.

Row 10: For **2nd triangle,** skip next 11 sts on rnd 9, join rust with sl st in next st, ch 1, sc first 2 sts tog, sc in next 9 sts, sc next 2 sts tog leaving remaining sts unworked, turn (11 sc).

Rows 11-16: Repeat same rows of first triangle.

For **3rd triangle,** using dk. brown, work same as 2nd triangle.

For **4th triangle,** work same as 2nd triangle.

Rnd 17: With right side facing you, working around entire outer edge, join med. brown with sc in first st of rnd 9 after any triangle, sc in next 10 sts, *[evenly space 8 sc in ends of rows across next triangle, (sc, ch 2, sc) in next corner ch-2 sp, evenly space 8 sc in ends of rows across same triangle], sc in next 11 sts; repeat from * 2 more times; repeat between [ ], join with sl st in first sc (29 sc across each side between corner ch-2 sps).

Rnd 18: Ch 1, sc in first st, ch 1, skip next st, *(sc in next st, ch 1, skip next st) across to

Square Dance

Continued from page 103

next corner ch sp, (sc, ch 3, sc) in next ch sp, ch 1, skip next st; repeat from * 3 more times, (sc in next st, ch 1, skip next st) 4 times, join, fasten off (16 sc and 15 ch-1 sps across each side between corner ch-3 sps).

Holding Squares wrong sides together, matching sts, with med. brown, sew together through **back lps** in 5 rows of 7 Squares each.

Border

Rnd 1: Working around entire outer edge, join med. brown with sc in first sc after any corner ch-3 sp, sc in each ch-1 sp, sc in each sc, sc in each ch sp on each side of seams and hdc in each seam around with (sc, ch 3, sc) in each corner ch-3 sp, join, **turn** (169 sts across each short end between corner ch sps, 237 sts across each long edge between corner ch sps).

Rnd 2: Ch 1, sc in first st, ch 1, skip next st, (sc, ch 3, sc) in next ch sp, ch 1, skip next st, *(sc in next st, ch 1, skip next st) across to next corner ch-3 sp, (sc, ch 3, sc) in next ch sp; repeat from * 2 more times, ch 1, skip next st, (sc in next st, ch 1, skip next st) across, join, **turn** (86 sc and 85 ch-1 sps across each short end between corner ch sps, 120 sc and 119 ch-1 sps across each long edge between corner ch sps).

Rnd 3: Ch 1, sc in each st and in each ch-1 sp around with (sc, ch 3, sc) in each corner ch-3 sp, join, **turn,** fasten off (173 sc across each short end between corner ch sps, 241 sc across each long edge between corner ch sps).

Rnd 4: With wrong side facing you, join rust with sc in first st, ch 1, skip next st, sc in next st, ch 1, skip next st, (sc, ch 3, sc) in next corner ch sp, *ch 1, skip next st, (sc in next st, ch 1, skip next st) across to next corner ch sp, (sc, ch 3, sc) in next ch sp; repeat from * 2 more times, ch 1, skip next st, (sc in next st, ch 1, skip next st) across, join, **turn** (88 sc and 87 ch-1 sps across each short end between corner ch sps, 122 sc and 121 ch-1 sps across each long edge between corner ch sps).

Rnd 5: Ch 3, dc in each ch-1 sp and in each sc around with (2 dc, ch 2, 2 dc) in each corner ch sp, join with sl st in top of ch-3, **turn** (179 dc across each short end between corner ch sps, 247 dc across each long edge between corner ch sps).

Rnd 6: Sl st in next st, ch 1, sc in same st, skip next st, (sc, ch 2, sc) in next st, skip next st, sc in next st, skip next st, [◊sc in next corner ch sp, (ch 2, sc) 3 times in same sp, skip next st, sc in next st, skip next st◊, *(sc, ch 2, sc) in next st, skip next st, sc in next st, skip next st*; repeat between ** across to next corner ch sp]; repeat between [ ] 2 more times; repeat between ◊◊; repeat between ** around to last 2 sts, (sc, ch 2, sc) in next st, skip last st, join, **turn,** fasten off.

Rnd 7: With right side facing you, join dk. brown with sc in center ch sp of any corner, ch 4, sc in 4th ch from hook, sc in same ch sp, [◊(sc, ch 3, sc) in next ch sp, *skip next st, sc in next st, (sc, ch 3, sc) in next ch-2 sp; repeat from * across◊ to center ch sp of next corner, (sc, ch 4, sc in 4th ch from hook, sc) in next ch sp]; repeat between [ ] 2 more times; repeat between ◊◊, join, fasten off. ✐

Rustic Cabins

Continued from page 100

Rnd 2: Ch 1, sc in each st around with (sc, ch 2, sc) in each corner ch sp, join, **turn,** fasten off.

Rnd 3: Join variegated A with sl st in any corner ch sp, ch 3, (dc, ch 2, 2 dc) in same sp, dc in each st around with (2 dc, ch 2, 2 dc) in each corner ch sp, join with sl st in top of ch-3, **turn.**

Rnd 4: Ch 3, dc in each st around with (2 dc, ch 2, 2 dc) in each corner ch sp, join, **turn,** fasten off.

Rnd 5: Join teal with sc in any corner ch sp, (sc, ch 2, 2 sc) in same sp, sc in each st around with (2 sc, ch 2, 2 sc) in each corner ch sp, join with sl st in first sc, **turn.**

Rnd 6: Repeat rnd 2.

Rnds 7-8: With variegated B, repeat rnds 3 and 4. ✑

Assembly Diagram

☐ = Rust
☐ = Teal
■ = Variegated A
☐ = Variegated B

Section Diagram

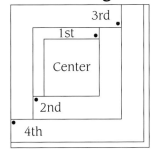

3rd
1st
Center
2nd
4th

• = Start section here.

Indian Summer

Continued from page 99

Edging

Rnd 1: Working around entire outer edge, join green with sc in any corner, sc in each st and in end of each row around with 3 sc in each corner, join with sl st in first sc.

Rnd 2: Ch 1; working left to right, **reverse sc** (see page 159) in each st around, join, fasten off. ✑

Section Diagram

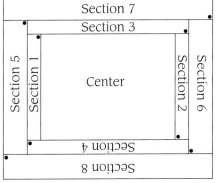

Section 7
Section 3
Section 5
Section 1
Center
Section 2
Section 6
Section 4
Section 8

• = Start section here

E Pluribus Unum

Designed by Sandra Miller Maxfield

Finished Size: 61" x 69" not including Fringe.

Materials: Worsted-weight yarn — 40 oz. aran fleck, 15 oz. navy fleck, 4 oz. maroon fleck, 3 oz. each green fleck and gold; tapestry needle; H hook or size needed to obtain gauge.

Gauge: 3 dc = 1"; 7 dc rows = 4".

Skill Level: ★★ Average

Afghan

Notes: Each square on graph equals 2 dc.

When changing colors (see page 159), always drop yarn to wrong side of work. Use a separate ball of yarn for each color section. Do not carry yarn across from one section to another. Fasten off colors at end of each color section.

Ch-3 at begining of rows is used and counted as first st.

Work odd-numbered graph rows from right to left; work even-numbered graph rows from left to right.

Row 1: With navy, ch 186, dc in 4th ch from hook, dc in each ch across, turn (184 dc).

Row 2: For **row 2 of graph** (see page 111), ch 3, dc in next st changing to aran in last st made, dc in each st across to last 2 sts changing to navy in last st made, dc in each of last 2 sts, turn.

Rows 3-121: Ch 3, dc in each st across changing colors according to graph, turn. At end of last row, fasten off.

With green, using Chain Stitch (see illustration), embroider 3 stems from small flowers to eagle's foot as shown in photo.

Chain Stitch

Fringe

For **each Fringe,** cut 4 strands navy each 17" long. Holding all strands together, fold in half, insert hook in st, draw all loose ends through fold, tighten. Trim ends.

Fringe in every other st across short ends of Afghan. ✐

Graph on page 111

Brave Image

Designed by Lynda Lefler-Wright

Finished Size: 54" x 60".

Materials: Worsted-weight yarn — 21 oz. black, 20 oz. tan, 17 oz. off-white, 6 oz. each red and blue; G hook or size needed to obtain gauge.

Gauge: Each Square = 3" square.

Skill Level: ★★ Average

Solid Square
(make 119 black, 89 off-white, 88 brown, 16 red and 8 blue)

Rnd 1: Ch 6, sl st in first ch to form ring, ch 3, 3 dc in ring, ch 2, (4 dc in ring, ch 2) 3 times, join with sl st in top of ch-3 (16 dc, 4 ch sps).

Rnd 2: Ch 3, dc in each st around with (2 dc, ch 2, 2 dc) in each ch sp, join, fasten off (32 dc, 4 ch sps).

Two-Color Diagonal Square
(make 10 red/blue, 6 tan/off-white, 4 red/black, 4 blue/black, 4 tan/black, 3 black/off-white, 3 blue/off-white)

Rnd 1: With first color, ch 6, sl st in first ch to form ring, ch 3, 3 dc in ring, ch 2, 4 dc in ring, ch 2 changing to 2nd color in last ch made (see illustration), (4 dc in ring, ch 2) 2 times changing to first color in last ch made, join with sl st in top of ch-3.

Chain Color Change

Rnd 2: Ch 3, dc in each of next 3 sts, (2 dc, ch 2, 2 dc) in next ch sp, dc in next 4 sts, (2 dc, ch 2) in next ch sp changing to 2nd color in last ch made, 2 dc in same ch sp, dc in next 4 sts, (2 dc, ch 2, 2 dc) in next ch sp, dc in next 4 sts, (2 dc, ch 2) in next ch sp changing to first color in last ch made, 2 dc in same ch sp, join, fasten off both colors.

Square A
(make 2)

Rnd 1: With tan, ch 6, sl st in first ch to form ring, ch 3, dc in ring, ch 2, 4 dc in ring, ch 2, 2 dc in ring changing to off-white (see page 159) in last st made, 2 dc in ring, ch 2, 4 dc in ring, ch 2, 2 dc in ring changing to tan in last st made, join with sl st in top of ch-3.

Rnd 2: Ch 3, dc in next st, *(2 dc, ch 2, 2 dc) in next ch sp, dc in next 4 sts, (2 dc, ch 2, 2 dc) in next ch sp, dc in each of next 2 sts* changing to off-white in last st made, dc in each of next 2 sts; repeat between **, join, fasten off both colors.

Square B

Rnd 1: With off-white, ch 6, sl st in first ch to form ring, ch 3, dc in ring, (ch 2, 4 dc in ring) 2 times, ch 2 changing to blue in last ch made, 4 dc in ring, ch 2, 2 dc in ring changing to off-white in last st made, join with sl st in top of ch-3.

Rnd 2: Ch 3, dc in next st, *(2 dc, ch 2, 2 dc) in next ch sp, dc in next 4 sts; repeat from *, (2 dc, ch 2) in next ch sp changing to blue in last ch made, 2 dc in same ch sp, dc in next 4 sts, (2 dc, ch 2, 2 dc) in next ch sp, dc in each of last 2 sts, join, fasten off both colors.

Square C

Rnd 1: With blue, ch 6, sl st in first ch to form ring, ch 3, dc in ring, ch 2, 4 dc in ring, ch 2 changing to off-white in last ch made, (4 dc in ring, ch 2) 2 times, 2 dc in ring changing to blue in last st made, join with sl st in top of ch-3.

Rnd 2: Ch 3, dc in next st, (2 dc, ch 2, 2 dc) in next ch sp, dc in next 4 sts, (2 dc, ch 2) in next ch sp changing to off-white in last st made, 2 dc in same ch sp, *dc in next 4 sts, (2 dc, ch 2, 2 dc) in next ch sp; repeat from *, dc in each of last 2 sts, join, fasten off both colors.

Brave Image

Continued from page 109

Square D

Rnd 1: With tan, ch 6, sl st in first ch to form ring, ch 3, 3 dc in ring, (ch 2, 4 dc in ring) 2 times, ch 2 changing to off-white in last st made, 4 dc in ring, ch 2 changing to tan in last ch made, join with sl st in top of ch-3.

Rnd 2: Ch 3, dc in each of next 3 sts, *(2 dc, ch 2, 2 dc) in next ch sp, dc in next 4 sts; repeat from *, (2 dc, ch 2) in next ch sp changing to off-white in last ch made, 2 dc in same ch sp, dc in next 4 sts, (2 dc, ch 2) in next ch sp changing to tan in last ch made, 2 dc in same ch sp, join, fasten off both colors.

Square E

Rnd 1: With off-white, ch 6, sl st in first ch to form ring, ch 3, 3 dc in ring, ch 2, 4 dc in ring, ch 2 changing to blue in last ch made, 4 dc in ring, ch 2 changing to red in last ch made, 4 dc in ring, ch 2 changing to off-white in last ch made, join with sl st in top of ch-3.

Rnd 2: Ch 3, dc in each of next 3 sts, (2 dc, ch 2, 2 dc) in next ch sp, dc in next 4 sts, (2 dc, ch 2) in next ch sp changing to blue in last ch made, 2 dc in same ch sp, dc in next 4 sts, (2 dc, ch 2) in next ch sp changing to red in last ch made, 2 dc in same ch sp, dc in next 4 sts, (2 dc, ch 2) in next ch sp changing to off-white in last ch made, 2 dc in same ch sp, join, fasten off all colors.

Assembly

Holding Squares wrong sides together, matching sts, changing colors as needed to match Squares, sc together according to Square Assembly Diagram.

Edging

Working around entire outer edge of Afghan, join black with sc in any corner ch sp, (sc, ch 2, 2 sc) in same sp, skipping seams, sc in each st and sc in each ch sp on each side of seams around with (2 sc, ch 2, 2 sc) in each corner ch sp, join with sl st in first sc, fasten off. ✍

Square Assembly Diagram

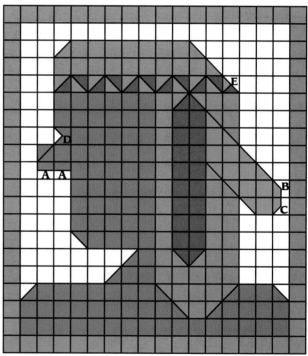

E Pluribus Unum

Instructions on page 106

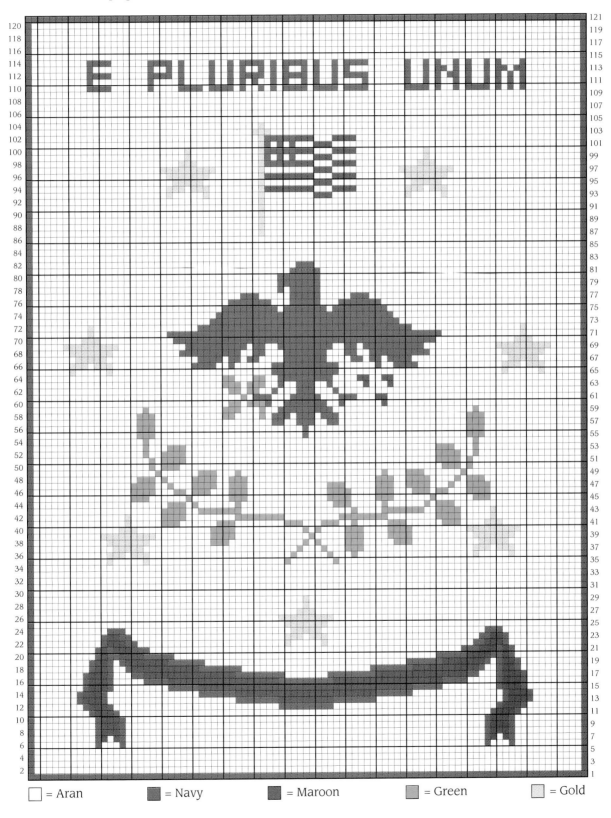

☐ = Aran   ■ = Navy   ■ = Maroon   ■ = Green   ☐ = Gold

Romantics

Embrace your passion for enchantment and allure when you escape to a world of classic lines and poetic designs that transcend your wildest dreams. Pamper your senses and caress your soul with a luxurious diversion from conventional decorating. From elegantly formal to pleasingly simple these captivating creations will capture your heart forever.

Milady's Lace

Designed by Maggie Weldon

Finished Size: 46" x 63" not including Fringe.

Materials: Sport-weight cotton yarn — 48 oz. off-white; tapestry needle; G hook or size needed to obtain gauge.

Gauge: Row 1 of Panel = 3⅜" wide; rows 1-4 of Panel = 2½". Each Panel is 6½" wide.

Skill Level: ★★ Average

Strip
(make 7)

Row 1: Ch 15, dc in 4th ch from hook, ch 2, skip next 2 chs, sc in next ch, ch 1, skip next ch, (dc, ch 1) 3 times in next ch, skip next ch, sc in next ch, ch 2, skip next 2 chs, dc in each of last 2 chs, turn (7 dc, 4 ch-1 sps, 2 ch-2 sps).

Notes: *For **popcorn (pc)**, 5 dc in next st or ch sp, drop lp from hook, insert hook in first st of 5-dc group, draw dropped lp through.*

Front of row 1 is wrong side of work.

Row 2: Ch 3, dc in next dc, skip next ch-2 sp, pc in next ch-1 sp, (ch 3, pc in next ch-1 sp) 3 times, dc in each of last 2 dc, turn (4 dc, 3 ch-3 sps).

Row 3: Ch 3, dc in next dc, ch 2, sc in next ch-3 sp, (ch 3, sc in next ch-3 sp) 2 times, ch 2, dc in each of last 2 dc, turn (4 dc, 2 ch-3 sps, 2 ch-2 sps).

Row 4: Ch 3, dc in next dc, ch 4, skip next ch-2 sp, sc in next ch-3 sp, ch 3, sc in next ch-3 sp, ch 4, skip next ch-2 sp, dc in each of last 2 dc, turn (4 dc, 2 ch-4 sps, 1 ch-3 sp).

Row 5: Ch 3, dc in next dc, ch 2, sc in next ch-4 sp, ch 1, (dc, ch 1) 3 times in next ch-3 sp, sc in next ch-4 sp, ch 2, dc in each of last 2 dc, turn (7 dc, 4 ch-1 sps, 2 ch-2 sps).

Rows 6-95: Repeat rows 2-5 consecutively, ending with row 3.

Rnd 96: Working around outer edge, ch 3, (dc, ch 2, 2 dc) in same st, dc in next dc, 2 dc in next ch-2 sp, 3 dc in each of next 2 ch-3 sps, 2 dc in next ch-2 sp, dc in next dc, (2 dc, ch 2, 2 dc) in last dc; *working in end of rows, dc in first row, 2 dc in each row across*; working in starting ch on opposite side of row 1, (2 dc, ch 2, 2 dc) in first ch, dc in next 5 chs, 2 dc in next ch, dc in next 5 chs, (2 dc, ch 2, 2 dc) in last ch; repeat between **, join with sl st in top of ch-3 (16 dc across each short end between corner ch-2 sps, 193 dc across each long side between corner ch-2 sps).

Rnd 97: Sl st in next st, sl st in next ch-2 sp, ch 3, (dc, ch 2, 2 dc) in same sp, *(ch 1, skip next st, pc in next st) 7 times, ch 1, skip next 2 sts, (2 dc, ch 2, 2 dc) in next ch-2 sp, (ch 1, skip next st, pc in next st) across to last st before next corner ch-2 sp, skip last st, ch 1*, (2 dc, ch 2, 2 dc) in next ch-2 sp; repeat between **, join (8 ch-1 sps and 7 pc across each short end between corners, 97 ch-1 sps and 96 pc across each long side between corners).

Rnd 98: Sl st in next st, sl st in next ch-2 sp, ch 6, dc in same sp, *[ch 1, dc in next st, (ch 1, skip next st, dc in next ch-1 sp) across to 2 sts before next corner ch-2 sp, ch 1, skip next st, dc in next st, ch 1], (dc, ch 3, dc) in next ch-2 sp; repeat from * 2 more times; repeat between [ ], join with sl st in 3rd ch of ch-6, fasten off.

Matching sts and ch sps, sew long edges of Strips together through **back lps** only.

Fringe

For **each Fringe,** cut 4 strands each 13" long. Holding all strands together, fold in half, insert hook in ch sp, draw fold through, draw all loose ends through fold, tighten. Trim ends.

Fringe in each ch sp across short ends of Afghan.

Marbled Elegance

Designed by Ellen Anderson

Finished Size: 51" x 72".

Materials: Worsted-weight yarn — 42 oz. aran fleck, 10 oz. black, 5 oz. gray and 4 oz. aran; H hook or size needed to obtain gauge.

Gauge: 7 sc = 2"; 7 sc **back lp** rows = 2".

Skill Level: ★★ Average

Afghan

Row 1: With aran fleck, ch 260; working in **back bar of chs** (see illustration), sc in 2nd ch from hook, sc in next 12 chs, 3 sc in next ch, sc in next 13 chs, (skip next 2 chs, sc in next 13 chs, 3 sc in next ch, sc in next 13 chs) across, turn (261 sc).

Back Bar of Chain

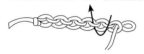

Rows 2-12: Working in **back lps** only, ch 1, skip first st, sc in next 13 sts, 3 sc in next st, (sc in next 13 sts, skip next 2 sts, sc in next 13 sts, 3 sc in next st) across to last 14 sts, sc in next 12 sts, skip next st, sc in last st, turn. At end of last row, fasten off.

Row 13: Working this row in **back lps** only, join black with sc in 2nd st, sc in next 12 sts, 3 sc in next st, (sc in next 13 sts, skip next 2 sts, sc in next 13 sts, 3 sc in next st) across to last 14 sts, sc in next 12 sts, skip next st, sc in last st, turn.

Row 14: Repeat row 2, **do not** turn, fasten off.

Row 15: Join gray with sc in 2nd st; for **puff st,** (yo, insert hook in same st, yo, draw lp through) 3 times, yo, draw through all 7 lps on hook; (skip next st, sc in next st, puff st) 6 times, (sc in next st, puff st) 2 times, (skip next st, sc in next st, puff st) 6 times, *skip next 2 sts, sc in next st, puff st, (skip next st, sc in next st, puff st) 6 times, (sc in next st, puff st) 2 times, (skip next st, sc in next st, puff st) 6 times; repeat from * across to last st, sc in last st, turn, fasten off (136 sc, 135 puff sts).

Row 16: Working this row in **back lps** only, join black with sc in 2nd st, skip next st, sc in next 12 sts, 3 sc in next st, (sc in next 13 sts, skip next 3 sts, sc in next 13 sts, 3 sc in next st) across to last 15 sts, sc in next 12 sts, skip next st, sc in next st, skip last st, turn (261 sc).

Row 17: Repeat row 2, fasten off.

Row 18: With aran fleck, repeat row 13.

Rows 19-29: Repeat row 2. At end of last row, fasten off.

Rows 30-31: Repeat rows 13 and 14.

Row 32: With aran, repeat row 15.

Rows 33-34: Repeat rows 16 and 17.

Row 35: With aran fleck, repeat row 13.

Rows 36-165: Repeat rows 2-35 consecutively, ending with row 29. At end of last row, fasten off. ✐

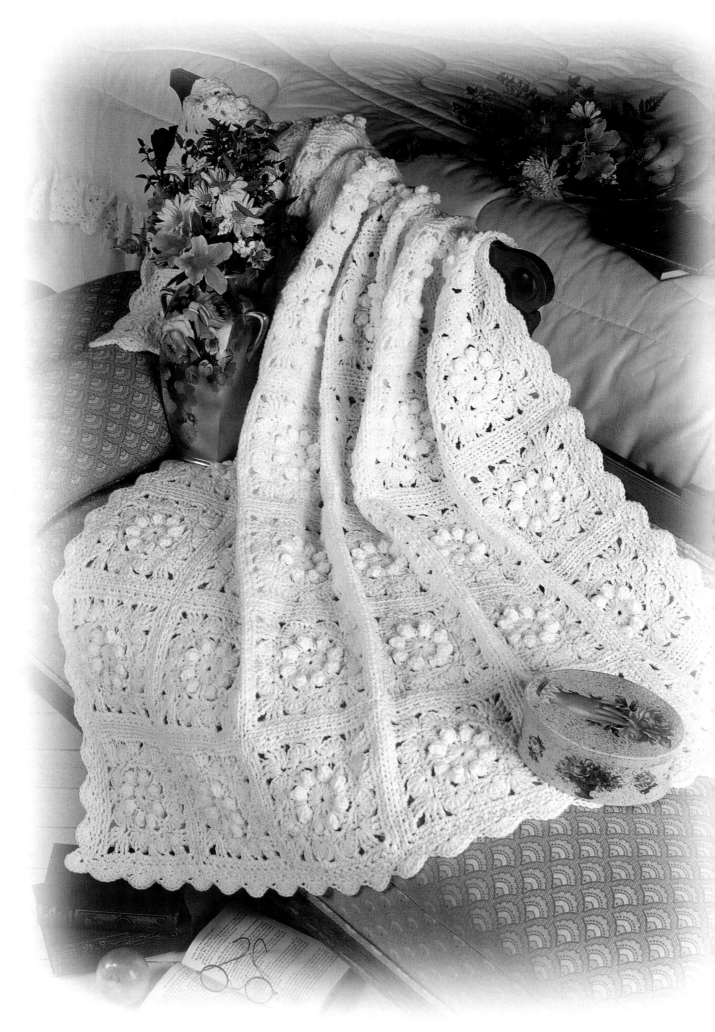

White on White

Designed by Katherine Eng

Finished Size: 46" x 68".

Materials: Worsted-weight yarn — 29 oz. white and 25 oz. off-white; tapestry needle; G hook or size needed to obtain gauge.

Gauge: Rnd 1 of Square = 1¾" across. Each Square is 7¼" square.

Skill Level: ★★ Average

Square
(make 54)

Rnd 1: With white, ch 4, sl st in first ch to form ring, ch 3, 15 dc in ring, join with sl st in top of ch-3 (16 dc).

Notes: *For **beginning popcorn (beg pc),** ch 3, 3 dc in same st, drop lp from hook, insert hook in top of ch-3, draw dropped lp through.*

*For **popcorn (pc),** 4 dc in next st, drop lp from hook, insert hook in first st of 4-dc group, draw dropped lp through.*

Rnd 2: Beg pc, ch 3, skip next st, (pc, ch 3, skip next st) around, join with sl st in top of beg pc, fasten off (8 pc, 8 ch sps).

Rnd 3: Join off-white with sc in any ch sp; working over same ch sp, tr in next skipped st of rnd 1, sc in same ch sp on this rnd, ch 2, *sc in next ch sp; working over same ch sp, tr in next skipped st of rnd 1, sc in same ch sp on this rnd, ch 2; repeat from * around, join with sl st in first sc (24 sts, 8 ch sps).

Rnd 4: Ch 1, sc in each st and 3 sc in each ch sp around, join, fasten off (48 sc).

Rnd 5: Join white with sc in 3rd st, skip next 2 sts; for **shell,** 7 dc in next st; skip next 2 sts, (sc in next st, skip next 2 sts, shell in next st, skip next 2 sts) around, join, fasten off (8 shells, 8 sc).

Rnd 6: Join off-white with sc in center dc of any shell, *[ch 2, 3 dc in next sc, ch 2, sc in center dc of next shell, ch 2; for **corner,** (3 tr, ch 3, 3 tr) in next sc; ch 2], sc in center dc of next shell; repeat from * 2 more times; repeat between [ ], join (44 sts, 16 ch-2 sps, 4 ch-3 sps).

Rnd 7: Ch 1, sc in each st and 2 sc in each ch-2 sp around with (2 sc, ch 2, 2 sc) in each corner ch-3 sp, join, fasten off (23 sc across each side between corner ch sps).

Rnd 8: Join white with sc in any corner ch sp, ch 3, sc in same sp, *[ch 1, skip next st, (sc in next st, ch 1, skip next st) across] to next corner ch sp, (sc, ch 3, sc) in next ch sp; repeat from * 2 more times; repeat between [ ], join, fasten off.

With white, matching sts and ch sps, sew Squares together through **back lps** in 6 rows of 9 Squares.

Border

Rnd 1: Working around outer edge, join white with sc in corner ch sp before one short end, ch 3, sc in same ch sp, sc in each st, in each ch sp and hdc in each seam around with (sc, ch 3, sc) in each corner ch sp, join with sl st in first sc, sl st in next ch-3 sp, **turn** (167 sts across each short end between corner ch sps, 251 sts across each long side between corner ch sps).

Rnd 2: Ch 1, sc in same ch sp, ch 1, skip next st, *(sc in next st, ch 1, skip next st) across to next corner ch sp, (sc, ch 3, sc) in next ch sp, ch 1, skip next st; repeat from * 3 more times, (sc in next st, ch 1, skip next st) across to next corner ch sp, sc in same ch sp as first sc, ch 3, join, **turn** (85 sc and 84 ch-1 sps across each short end between corner ch-3 sps, 127 sc and 126 ch-1 sps across each long side between corner ch-3 sps).

Rnd 3: Sl st in first corner ch sp, ch 3, 8 dc in same sp, *sc in next sc, (skip next sc, shell in next sc, skip next sc, sc in next sc) across to next corner ch sp, 9 dc in next ch sp, skip next sc, sc in next sc, skip next sc, (shell in next sc, skip next sc, sc in next sc, skip next sc) across to next corner ch sp*, 9 dc in next ch sp; repeat between **, join with sl st in top of ch-3, fasten off. ✑

Evergreen Classic

Designed by Daisy Watson

Finished Size: 50" x 76".

Materials: Worsted-weight yarn — 56 oz. spruce; I hook or size needed to obtain gauge.

Gauge: 3 dc = 1"; 3 dc rows = 2".

Skill Level: ★★ Average

Afghan

Note: Back of row 1 is right side of work.

Row 1: Ch 144, hdc in 3rd ch from hook, hdc in each ch across, turn (143 hdc).

Row 2: Ch 3, dc in each of next 2 sts, ch 1, skip next st, dc in next 15 sts, ch 1, skip next st, dc in each of next 3 sts, (ch 1, skip next st, dc in next 15 sts, ch 1, skip next st, dc in each of next 3 sts) across, turn (129 dc, 14 ch-1 sps).

Row 3: Ch 3, dc in each of next 2 sts, ch 1, skip next ch-1 sp, dc in next 15 sts, ch 1, skip next ch-1 sp, dc in each of next 3 sts, (ch 1, skip next ch-1 sp, dc in next 15 sts, ch 1, skip next ch-1 sp, dc in each of last 3 sts) across, turn.

Row 4: Ch 3, dc in each of next 2 sts, ch 1, skip next ch-1 sp, (dc in next st, ch 1, skip next st or ch-1 sp) across to last 3 sts, dc in each of last 3 sts, turn (74 dc, 69 ch-1 sps).

Row 5: Ch 3, dc in each of next 2 sts, ch 1, skip next ch-1 sp, dc in next 15 sts and ch-1 sps, ch 1, skip next ch-1 sp, (dc in each of next 3 sts and ch-1 sps, ch 1, skip next ch-1 sp, dc in next 15 sts and ch-1 sps, ch 1, skip next ch-1 sp) across to last 3 sts, dc in each of last 3 sts, turn.

Row 6: Repeat row 3.

Notes: *For* **treble crochet cluster (tr cl),** *yo 2 times, insert hook in next st, yo, draw lp through, (yo, draw through 2 lps on hook) 2 times, *yo 2 times, insert hook in same st, yo, draw lp through, (yo, draw through 2 lps on hook) 2 times; repeat from *, yo, draw through all 4 lps on hook.*

For **double crochet cluster (dc cl),** *yo, insert hook in next st, yo, draw lp through, yo,*

draw through 2 lps on hook, *yo, insert hook in same st, yo, draw through 2 lps on hook; repeat from *, yo, draw through all 4 lps on hook.

Row 7: Ch 3, dc in each of next 2 sts, *ch 1, skip next ch-1 sp, dc in each of next 2 sts, ch 3, skip next st, tr cl in next st, skip next 3 sts, dc cl in next st, skip next 3 sts, tr cl in next st, ch 3, skip next st, dc in each of next 2 sts, ch 1, skip next ch-1 sp, dc in each of next 3 sts; repeat from * across, turn (52 dc, 14 tr cls, 14 ch-3 sps, 14 ch-1 sps, 7 dc cls).

Row 8: Ch 3, dc in each of next 2 sts, *ch 1, skip next ch-1 sp, dc in each of next 2 sts, ch 3, skip next ch-3 sp, sc in top of each of next 3 cls, ch 3, skip next ch-3 sp, dc in each of next 2 sts, ch 1, skip next ch-1 sp, dc in each of next 3 sts; repeat from * across, turn.

Row 9: Ch 3, dc in each of next 2 sts, *ch 1, skip next ch-1 sp, dc in each of next 2 sts, ch 1, skip next ch-3 sp, tr cl in next st, ch 3, dc cl in next st, ch 3, tr cl in next st, ch 1, skip next ch-3 sp, dc in each of next 2 sts, ch 1, skip next ch-1 sp, dc in each of next 3 sts; repeat from * across, turn.

Row 10: Ch 3, dc in each of next 2 sts, *ch 1, skip next ch-1 sp, dc in each of next 2 sts, dc in next ch-1 sp, dc in next cl, (3 dc in next ch-3 sp, dc in next cl) 2 times, dc in next ch-1 sp, dc in each of next 2 sts, ch 1, skip next ch-1 sp, dc in each of next 3 sts; repeat from * across, turn (129 dc, 14 ch-1 sps).

Rows 11-110: Repeat rows 3-10 consecutively, ending with row 6.

Row 111: Ch 2, hdc in each st and in each ch sp across, turn, fasten off.

Edging

Row 1: For **first side,** with right side facing you, working in end of rows across one long side, join with sc in row 1, (ch 1, sc in next row) across to last row, sl st in last row,

Continued on page 129

Gothic Romance

Designed by Maggie Weldon

Finished Size: 46" x 59".

Materials: Worsted-weight yarn — 40 oz. natural and 16 oz. green; tapestry needle; G hook or size needed to obtain gauge.

Gauge: 4 dc = 1"; 5 dc rows = 3"; 5 cr sts = 3"; 5 cr st rows = 3".

Skill Level: ★★ Average

Panel A
(make 3)

Row 1: With natural, ch 34, dc in 4th ch from hook, dc in each ch across, turn (32 dc).

Row 2: Ch 3, dc in each st across, turn.

Notes: *When changing colors (see page 159), always drop yarn to wrong side of work. Use a separate ball of yarn for each color section. **Do not** carry dropped color across more than 4 or 5 sts to next section of same color.*

Work odd-numbered rows on graph from right to left, work even-numbered rows on graph from left to right.

Row 3: For **row 3 of graph,** ch 3, dc in next 11 sts changing to green in last st made, dc in next 4 sts changing to natural in last st made, dc in each st across, turn.

Rows 4-26: Ch 3, dc in each st across changing colors according to graph, turn.

Rows 27-112: Ch 3, dc in each st across changing colors according to rows 5-26 on graph consecutively, turn, ending with row 24.

Row 113: Ch 3, dc in each of next 3 sts changing to green in last st made, dc in each of next 2 sts changing to natural in last st made, dc in each st across, turn.

Row 114: Ch 3, dc in next 25 sts changing to green in last st made, dc in each of next 2 sts changing to natural in last st made, dc in last 4 sts, turn. Fasten off green.

Rnd 115: For **edging,** work-

ing around outer edge, ch 3, (dc, ch 2, 2 dc) in same st, dc in each st across to last st, (2 dc, ch 2, 2 dc) in last st, 2 dc in end of each row across to next corner; working in starting ch on opposite side of row 1, (2 dc, ch 2, 2 dc) in first ch, dc in each ch across to last ch, (2 dc, ch 2, 2 dc) in last ch, 2 dc in end of each row across, join with sl st in top of ch-3, fasten off (34 dc across each short end between corner ch sps, 232 dc across each long side between corner ch sps).

Panel B
(make 2)

Note: For **cross stitch (cr st),** *skip next ch or st, dc in next ch or st; working over dc just made, dc in skipped ch or st.*

Row 1: With natural, ch 28, dc in 5th ch from hook; working over dc just made, dc in 4th ch from hook (first cr st made), cr st across to last ch, dc in last ch, turn (12 cr sts, 2 dc).

Rows 2-114: Ch 3, cr st across to last st, dc in last st, turn.

Rnd 115: For **edging,** working around outer edge, ch 3, (dc, ch 2, 2 dc) in same st, dc in each dc of each cr st across to last dc, (2 dc, ch 2, 2 dc) in last dc; *working in end of rows, 2 dc in each row across to next corner*; working in starting ch on opposite side of row 1, (2 dc, ch 2, 2 dc) in first ch, dc in each ch across to last ch, (2 dc, ch 2, 2 dc) in last ch; repeat between **, join with sl st in top of ch-3, fasten off (28 dc across each short end between corner ch sps, 232 dc across each long side between corner ch sps).

Graph

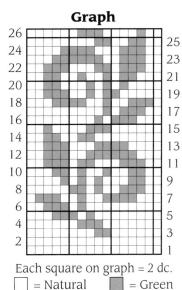

Each square on graph = 2 dc.

☐ = Natural   ■ = Green

Continued on page 129

Leaves of Gold

Designed by Rena Stevens

Finished Size: 44" x 47" not including Fringe.

Materials: Worsted-weight yarn — 18 oz. yellow and 14 oz. off-white; tapestry needle; I and J hooks or sizes needed to obtain gauges.

Gauges: With **I hook,** 2 cls and 1 ch-1 sp = 1"; 5 cls rows = 3". With **J hook,** 7 sc = 2"; 3 sc **back lp** rows = 1".

Skill Level: ★★ Average

Afghan

*Note: For **cluster (cl),** yo, insert hook in same ch or st as last st, yo, draw lp through, yo, draw through 2 lps on hook, skip next ch or st, yo, insert hook in next ch or st, yo, draw lp through, yo, draw through 2 lps on hook, yo, draw through all 3 lps on hook.*

Row 1: For **row 1 of graph** (see page 129), with I hook and yellow, ch 35 changing to off-white in last ch made, ch 64 changing to yellow in last st made, ch 39, yo, insert hook in 5th ch from hook, yo, draw lp through, yo, draw through 2 lps on hook, skip next ch, yo, insert hook in next ch, yo, draw lp through, yo, draw through 2 lps on hook, yo, draw through all 3 lps on hook (first cl made), (ch 1, cl) 16 times changing to off-white in last st made (see page 159), (ch 1, cl) 32 times changing to yellow in last st made, (ch 1, cl) 17 times, ch 1, dc in last ch, turn (67 ch-1 sps, 66 cls, 2 dc).

Rows 2-18: Changing colors according to corresponding row on graph, ch 4, cl, (ch 1, cl) across to last st, ch 1, dc in last st, turn.

Rows 19-78: Repeat rows 2-18 consecutively, ending with row 14. At end of last row, fasten off.

Surface Chain

With J hook and 2 strands yellow held together, holding yarn behind Afghan, working from bottom to top in ch-1 sps between color changes, place slip knot on hook, drop lp from hook, insert hook through Afghan in row 1, draw dropped lp through (first sl st made), sl st in ch-1 sp of each row across, fasten off.

Repeat in ch-1 sps along color changes on other side.

Leaf
(make 8 each off-white and yellow)

Note: Front of row 1 is wrong side of work.

Row 1: With J hook, ch 19, sc in 2nd ch from hook, sc in each ch across to last ch; for **point,** 3 sc in last ch; working on opposite side of ch, sc in each ch across, turn (37 sc).

Rows 2-9: Working these rows in **back lps** only, ch 1, skip first st, sc in each st across to point, sc in next st, 3 sc in next st, sc in next st, sc in each st across leaving last 3 sts unworked, turn. At end of last row, fasten off.

Sew Leaves to Afghan as shown in Placement Diagram, overlapping bottom point of each Leaf over Surface Chain.

Leaf Placement Diagram

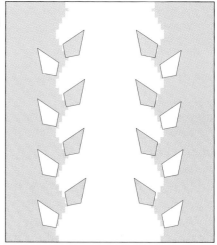

Fringe

For **each Fringe,** cut 10 strands yellow each 15" long. Holding all strands together, fold in half, insert hook in st, draw fold through, draw all ends through fold, tighten. Trim ends.

Fringe in each corner and in every 4th st across short ends of Afghan. ✍

Graph on page 129

Greek Silhouette

Designed by Tammy Cromer–Campbell for T&S Designs

Finished Size: 55" x 73".

Materials: Worsted-weight yarn — 45 oz. tan and 25 oz. black; I hook or size needed to obtain gauge.

Gauge: 3 sts = 1"; 3 tr rows and 2 sc rows worked in pattern = 3".

Skill Level: ★★★ Advanced

Afghan

Notes: *Color change graph shows only odd-numbered rows. Even-numbered sc rows are not shown on graph.*

When changing colors (see page 159), always drop yarn to wrong side of work. Carry dropped color across back of work to next section of same color. **Do not** *carry black across center section of afghan.*

For **popcorn (pc),** *5 tr in next st, drop lp from hook, insert hook in top of first tr of 5-tr group, draw dropped lp through.*

For **cross stitch (cr st),** *skip next st, tr in next st; working behind tr just made, tr in skipped st.*

Ch-4 at beginning of odd-numbered rows counts as first tr.

Back of row 1 is right side of work.

Row 1: With black, ch 167, tr in 5th ch from hook, tr in each ch across, turn (164 tr).

Row 2: Ch 1, sc in each st across, turn.

Row 3: For **row 3 of graph** (see page 128), ch 4, tr in each of next 2 sts, pc in next st, tr in next st, pc in next st changing to tan, tr in next 12 sts changing to black in last st made, (tr in next st, pc in next st) 2 times, *(tr in next st, pc in next st) 2 times changing to tan in last st made, tr in next 12 sts changing to black in last st made, (tr in next st, pc in next st) 4 times changing to tan in last st made, tr in next 12 sts changing to black in last st made, (tr in next st, pc in next st) 2 times; repeat from * 2 more times, (tr in next st, pc in next st) 2 times changing to tan in last st made, tr in next 12 sts changing to black in last st made, (tr in next st, pc in next st) 2 times, tr in each of last 2 sts, turn (132 tr, 32 pc).

Row 4: Changing colors according to color pattern established on last row, ch 1, sc in each st across, turn (164 sc).

Row 5: Work according to corresponding row on graph, turn.

Rows 6-23: Repeat rows 4 and 5 alternately.

Row 24: Changing colors according to color pattern established on last row, ch 1, sc in first 24 sts changing to tan in last st made; sc in each st across to last 24 sts changing to black in last st made; changing colors according to color pattern established on last row, sc in last 24 sts, turn.

Row 25: Work according to corresponding row on graph across first 24 sts changing to tan in last st made; for center (see graph), tr in each st across to last 24 sts changing to black in last st made; work according to graph, turn.

Row 26: Repeat row 24.

Row 27: Work according to corresponding row on graph across to center changing to tan in last st made; (tr in next st, cr st) across to last 2 sts of center, tr in each of next 2 sts changing to black; work remainder of row according to same row on graph, turn.

Row 28: Repeat row 24.

Row 29: Repeat row 25.

Row 30: Repeat row 24.

Row 31: Work according to corresponding row on graph across to center changing to tan in last st made; tr in each of next 2 sts, (cr st, tr in next st) across center changing to black in last st made; work remainder of row according to same row on graph, turn.

Rows 32-97: Repeat rows 24-31 consecutively, ending with row 25.

Rows 98-121: Repeat rows 4 and 5 alternately. At end of last row, fasten off tan only.

Rnd 122: Working in sts and in ends of rows around outer edge, evenly spacing sts so piece lays flat, ch 1, sc around with 3 sc in each corner, join with sl st in first sc, fasten off. ✎

Graph on page 128

Graph

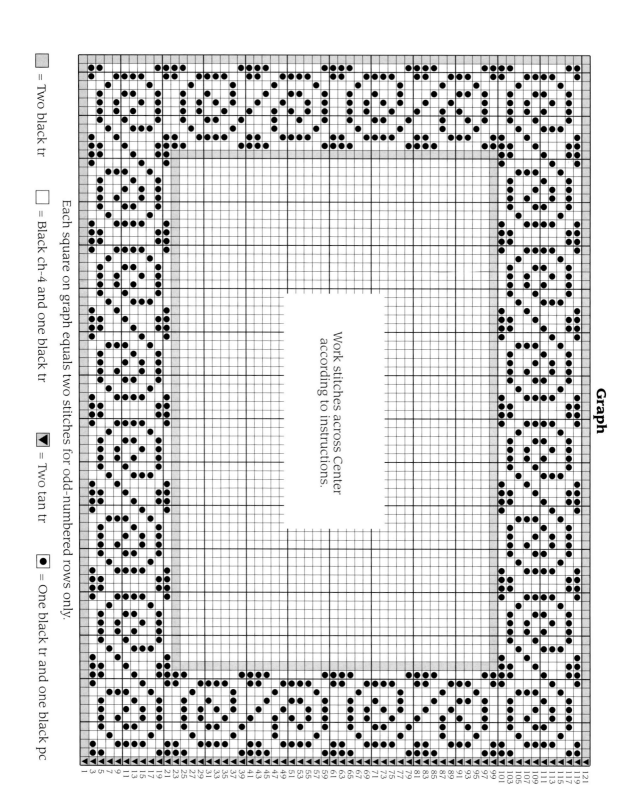

Work stitches across Center
according to instructions.

Each square on graph equals two stitches for odd-numbered rows only.

☐ = Two black tr

☐ = Black ch-4 and one black tr

▼ = Two tan tr

● = One black tr and one black pc

Leaves of Gold

Instructions on page 124

Graph

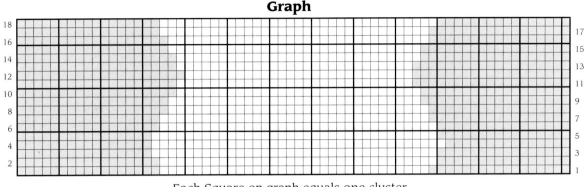

Each Square on graph equals one cluster.

☐ = Yellow   ☐ = Off-White

Gothic Romance

Continued from page 123

Alternating Panels, matching sts, sew long sides of Panels together through **back lps** only.

Border

Working around entire outer edge, join natural with sl st in any corner ch sp, ch 3, (dc, ch 2, 2 dc) in same sp, dc in each st and in each ch sp before and after seams around with (2 dc, ch 2, 2 dc) in each corner ch sp, join with sl st in top of ch-3, fasten off.

Evergreen Classic

Continued from page 120

fasten off; for **2nd side,** with right side facing you, working in end of rows across opposite long side, join with sl st in row 111, sc in next row, (ch 1, sc in next row) across, fasten off (110 sc and 109 ch-1 sps across each side).

Rnd 2: Working around outer edge, join with sc in first st of row 111, *(ch 4, sc in 4th ch from hook, ch 2, sc) 2 times in same st, ch 4, sc in 4th ch from hook, skip next 3 sts, (sc in next st, ch 4, sc in 4th ch from hook, ch 2, skip next 2 sts) across to last st before corner, sc in last st, (ch 4, sc in 4th ch from hook, ch 2, sc) 2 times in same st; working across side, skip next 3 sts or chs, (sc in next st or ch, ch 4, sc in 4th ch from hook, ch 2, skip next 2 sts or chs) across to next corner*; working in starting ch on opposite side of row 1, sc in first ch; repeat between **, join with sl st in first sc, fasten off.

Tidings

Joyous celebrations and sentimental memories fill the yuletide season with happiness beyond compare. Bring your colorful gift of warmth to the holidays with heavenly afghans that will gladden the hearts of young and old alike. As inviting to behold as a crackling fire and presents under the tree, these are designs that will keep them coming home year after year.

Holly Patch

Designed by Martha Brooks Stein

Finished Size: 41" x 56".

Materials: Worsted-weight yarn — 28 oz. white, 11 oz. green and 2½ oz. red; tapestry needle; H and I crochet hooks or sizes needed to obtain gauges.

Gauges: With **H hook,** 7 dc = 2"; 2 dc rows = 1". With **I hook,** each Square = 2½" across.

Skill Level: ★★ Average

Solid Square
(make 143 white, 48 green and 8 red)

Rnd 1: With l hook, ch 4, sl st in first ch to form ring, ch 3, 2 dc in ring, ch 2, (3 dc in ring, ch 2) 3 times, join with sl st in top of ch-3 (12 dc, 4 ch sps).

Rnd 2: Ch 3, dc in each st around with (2 dc, ch 2, 2 dc) in each ch sp, join, fasten off (28 dc, 4 ch sps).

Two–Color Square
(make 48)

Rnd 1: With I hook and white, ch 4, sl st in first ch to form ring, ch 3, (2 dc, ch 2, 3 dc) in ring, ch 1 changing to green (see illustration), ch 1, (3 dc, ch 2, 3 dc) in ring, ch 1 changing to white, ch 1, join with sl st in top of ch-3.

Chain
Color Change

Rnd 2: Ch 3, dc in each of next 2 sts, *2 dc, ch 2, 2 dc) in next ch sp, dc in each of next 3 sts, 2 dc in next ch sp*, ch 1 changing to green, ch 1, 2 dc in same ch sp as last 2 dc, dc in each of next 3 sts; repeat between **, ch 1 changing to white, ch 1, 2 dc in same ch sp, join, fasten off.

Holding Squares wrong sides together, matching sts, with matching color, sew together through **back lps** according to Square Assembly Diagram (see page 138).

Border

Rnd 1: Working around entire outer edge, in **back lps** only, with H hook and white, join with sc in first ch of corner ch sp before one short end, *[ch 2, sc in 2nd ch of same sp, sc in each st and in each ch sp across to next corner ch sp], sc in first ch of next corner ch sp; repeat from * 2 more times; repeat between [ ], join with sl st in first sc, fasten off (117 sc across each short end between corner ch sps, 171 sc across each long edge between corner ch sps).

Rnd 2: Join red with sl st in first corner ch sp, ch 3, (dc, ch 2, 2 dc) in same sp, dc in each st around with (2 dc, ch 2, 2 dc) in each corner ch sp, join with sl st in top of ch-3, fasten off (121 dc across each short end between ch sps, 175 dc across each long edge between ch sps).

Rnd 3: Join white with sl st in first ch sp, ch 3, (dc, ch 2, 2 dc) in same sp, dc in each st around with (2 dc, ch 2, 2 dc) in each corner ch sp, join (125 dc across each short end between ch sps, 179 dc across each long edge between ch sps).

Rnd 4: Sl st in next st, ch 3, *(2 dc, ch 2, 2 dc) in next ch sp, dc in each of next 2 sts, ch 1, skip next st, (dc in each of next 3 sts, ch 1, skip next st) across to 2 sts before next corner ch sp, dc in each of next 2 sts, (2 dc, ch 2, 2 dc) in next ch sp, dc in next st, ch 1, skip next st, (dc in each of next 3 sts, ch 1, skip next st) across to last st before next corner ch sp*, dc in next st; repeat between **, join.

Rnd 5: Ch 3, dc in each st and in each ch sp around with (2 dc, ch 2, 2 dc) in each corner ch-2 sp, join, fasten off (133 dc across each short end between ch sps, 187 dc across each long edge between ch sps).

Rnd 6: With green, repeat rnd 2 (137 dc across each short end between ch sps, 191 dc across each long edge between ch sps).

Rnds 7-9: Repeat rnds 3-5, ending with 141 dc across each short end between ch sps and 199 dc across each long edge between ch

Continued on page 138

Wreaths o' Lace

Designed by Ruth Owens

Finished Size: 42" x 62".

Materials: Worsted-weight yarn — 16 oz. white, 8 oz. each red and green, 4 oz. black; I crochet hook or size needed to obtain gauge.

Gauge: Rnds 1-4 of Block = 3¾" x 4". Each Block is 10" square.

Skill Level: ★★ Average

First Row
First Block

Rnd 1: With red, ch 2, 8 sc in 2nd ch from hook, join with sl st in first sc (8 sc).

Rnd 2: Ch 3, (tr, 2 dc) in same st, sc in next st, 3 dc in next st, sc in next st, (2 dc, tr, 2 dc) in next st, sc in next st, 3 dc in next st, sc in next st, dc in same st as first st, join with sl st in top of ch-3 (20 sts).

Rnd 3: Ch 1, sc in first st, 3 sc in next st, (sc in next 4 sts, 3 sc in next st) 3 times, sc in each of last 3 sts, join with sl st in first sc (28 sc).

Rnd 4: Ch 1, sc in each of first 2 sts, 3 sc in next st, (sc in next 6 sts, 3 sc in next st) 3 times, sc in last 4 sts, join, fasten off (36).

Notes: *For **beginning horizontal cluster (beg hcl),** *yo, insert hook in 3rd ch from hook, yo, draw lp through, yo, draw through 2 lps on hook; repeat from * in same ch, yo, draw through all 3 lps on hook.*

*For **horizontal cluster (hcl),** ch 2, *yo, insert hook in top of last st made, yo, draw lp through, yo, draw through 2 lps on hook; repeat from * in same st, yo, draw through all 3 lps on hook.*

Rnd 5: Join white with sl st in first st, ch 5, beg hcl, skip next 2 sts, *(dc, hcl) 3 times in next st, skip next 2 sts, (dc in next st, hcl, skip next 2 sts) 2 times, (dc, hcl) 2 times in next st, skip next 2 sts*, (dc in next st, hcl, skip next 2 sts) 2 times; repeat between **, dc in next st, hcl, skip last 2 sts, join with sl st in 3rd ch of ch-5, fasten off (18 dc, 18 hcls).

Rnd 6: Join green with sc in first dc, ch 4, skip next hcl, (sc in next dc, ch 4, skip next hcl) around, join with sl st in first sc.

Note: *For **shell,** (2 dc, ch 3, 2 dc) in next ch sp.*

Rnd 7: Ch 3, *2 dc in next ch sp, dc in next st, 2 dc in next ch sp, ch 4, sc in next st, ch 4, (2 dc in next ch sp, dc in next st) 2 times, shell in next ch sp, dc in next st, 2 dc in next ch sp, dc in next st, ch 4, sc in next ch sp, ch 4, dc in next st, 2 dc in next ch sp, dc in next st, shell in next ch sp*, dc in next st; repeat between **, join with sl st in top of ch-3 (40 dc, 8 ch sps, 4 shells, 4 sc).

Rnd 8: Ch 3, dc in next 4 sts, *ch 4, (sc in next ch sp, ch 4) 2 times, skip next st, dc in next 5 sts, shell in ch sp of next shell, skip next 2 sts of same shell, dc in next 4 sts, ch 4, (sc in next ch sp, ch 4) 2 times, dc in next 4 sts, shell in ch sp of next shell, skip next 2 sts of same shell*, dc in next 5 sts; repeat between **, join with sl st in top of ch-3, fasten off (36 dc, 24 ch sps).

Notes: *For **treble cluster (tr-cl),** *yo 2 times, insert hook in next ch sp, yo, draw lp through, (yo, draw through 2 lps on hook) 2 times; repeat from * 2 more times in same ch sp, yo, draw through all 4 lps on hook.*

*For **tr-cl-shell,** tr-cl in next ch sp, hcl in top of tr-cl just made, hcl in top of hcl just made, tr-cl in same ch sp.*

Rnd 9: Join white with sl st in first st, ch 5, beg hcl, *skip next 2 sts, dc in next st, hcl, (sc in next ch sp, hcl) 3 times, skip next st, dc in next st, hcl, skip next 2 sts, dc in next st, hcl, tr-cl-shell in next shell, hcl, skip next 2 sts of same shell, dc in next st, hcl, skip next 2 sts, dc in next st, hcl, (sc in next ch sp, hcl) 3 times, dc in next st, hcl, skip next 2 sts, dc in next st, hcl, tr-cl-shell in next shell, hcl*, dc in next st, hcl; repeat between **, join with sl st in 3rd ch of ch-5, fasten off (28 sts, 4 tr-cl-shells).

Continued on page 139

Victorian Poinsettia

Designed by Maggie Weldon

Finished Size: 58" x 69½".

Materials: Worsted-weight yarn — 42 oz. white, 21 oz. red, 14 oz. green and 3½ oz. yellow; tapestry needle; I crochet hook or size needed to obtain gauge.

Gauge: 3 dc = 1"; 3 dc rows = 2"; rnd 1 of Octagon = 2" across. Each Octagon is 11¼" across. Each Square is 4¾" across.

Skill Level: ★★ Average

Octagon
(make 30)

Note: For **popcorn (pc),** 3 dc in next ch sp, drop lp from hook, insert hook in first dc of 3-dc group, pick up dropped lp, draw through st.

Rnd 1: With yellow, ch 6, sl st in first ch to form ring, ch 3, pc in ring, (dc in ring, pc in ring) 7 times, join with sl st in top of ch-3, fasten off (8 pc, 8 dc).

Rnd 2: For **petals,** join red with sc in any dc, ch 6, skip next pc, (sc in next dc, ch 6, skip next pc) around, join with sl st in first sc (8 ch sps).

Note: For **picot,** ch 3, sl st in 3rd ch from hook.

Rnd 3: *3 dc in next ch sp, (picot, 3 dc) 5 times in same sp, sl st in same sp; repeat from * around, join with sl st in top of first dc, fasten off (8 petals).

Rnd 4: Working behind petals, join white with sl st in any skipped pc on rnd 1, ch 5, dc in same st, (dc, ch 2, dc) in each pc around, join with sl st in 3rd ch of ch-5 (8 ch sps).

Rnd 5: Sl st in first ch sp, ch 5, dc in same sp, ch 1, *(dc, ch 2, dc) in next ch sp, ch 1; repeat from * around, join (8 ch-2 sps, 8 ch-1 sps).

Rnd 6: Ch 3, (dc, ch 2, dc) in next ch-2 sp, dc in next st, dc in next ch-1 sp, *dc in next st, (dc, ch 2, dc) in next ch-2 sp, dc in next st, dc in next ch-1 sp; repeat from * around, join with sl st in top of ch-3 (40 dc, 8 ch sps).

Rnd 7: Ch 3, dc in next st, dc in next ch sp and in back of center picot on next petal at same time, ch 2, dc in same ch sp on this Motif; *dc in each st across to next ch sp, dc in next ch sp and in back of center picot on next petal at same time, ch 2, dc in same ch sp on this Motif; repeat from * 6 more times, dc in each of last 3 sts, join (56 dc, 8 ch sps).

Rnd 8: Ch 3, dc in each st around with (dc, ch 2, dc) in each ch sp, join (72 dc, 8 ch sps).

Notes: For **beginning V-st,** ch 4, dc in same st or ch sp.

For **V-st,** (dc, ch 1, dc) in next st or ch sp.

Rnd 9: Sl st in each of next 2 sts, beg V-st, *[skip next st, (dc, ch 2, dc) in next ch sp, skip next st, (V-st in next st, skip next 2 sts) 2 times], V-st in next st; repeat from * 6 more times; repeat between [ ], join with sl st in 3rd ch of ch-4 (24 V-sts, 8 ch-2 sps).

Rnd 10: Sl st in first ch sp, beg V-st, ch 1, (dc, ch 2, dc) in next ch-2 sp, *ch 1, (V-st in ch sp of next V-st, ch 1) across to next ch-2 sp, (dc, ch 2, dc) in next ch-2 sp; repeat from * 6 more times, ch 1, (V-st in ch sp of next V-st, ch 1) across, join, fasten off (32 ch-1 sps, 24 V-sts, 16 dc, 8 ch-2 sps).

Rnd 11: Join green with sc in any ch-2 sp, 2 sc in same sp, *[sc in next 6 sts and ch-1 sps, skip next st, sc in each of next 3 sts and ch-1 sp, skip next st, sc in next 4 sts and ch-1 sps], 3 sc in next corner ch-2 sp; repeat from * 6 more times; repeat between [ ], join with sl st in first sc, fasten off (13 sc across each side between 3-sc corners).

Leaf
(make 60)

With green, ch 16, sl st in 4th ch from hook, [*skip next 2 chs, dc in next ch, (picot, dc in same ch) 3 times, skip next 2 chs*, sl st in next ch; repeat between **], (sl st, ch 1, sl st) in last ch; working on opposite side of ch; repeat between [ ], sl st in last ch leaving long end for sewing, fasten off.

Sew 2 leaves to each Octagon as shown in photo.

Continued on page 138

Victorian Poinsettia

Continued from page 136

Square
(make 20)

Rnd 1: With white, ch 3, sl st in first ch to form ring, ch 6, (V-st in ring, ch 3) 3 times, dc in ring, ch 1, join with sl st in 3rd ch of ch-6 (4 V-sts, 4 ch-3 sps).

Rnd 2: Sl st in first ch-3 sp, beg V-st, ch 3, V-st in same sp, ch 1, *(V-st, ch 3, V-st) in next ch-3 sp, ch 1; repeat from * around, join with sl st in 3rd ch of ch-4 (4 ch-3 sps, 4 ch-1 sps).

Rnd 3: Sl st in next ch-1 sp, sl st in next st, sl st in next ch-3 sp, ch 5, (dc, ch 3, dc, ch 2, dc) in same sp, ch 1, skip next V-st, V-st in next ch-1 sp, ch 1, skip next V-st, *(dc, ch 2, dc, ch 3, dc, ch 2, dc) in next ch-3 sp, ch 1, skip next V-st, V-st in next ch-1 sp, ch 1, skip next V-st; repeat from * around, join with sl st in 3rd ch of ch-5, fasten off.

Rnd 4: Join green with sc in any corner ch-3 sp, 2 sc in same sp, sc in each st, sc in each ch-1 sp and 2 sc in each ch-2 sp around with 3 sc in each corner ch-3 sp, join with sl st in first sc, fasten off (15 sc across each side between center corner sts).

With green, matching sts, sew Octagons and Squares together through **back lps** according to Assembly Diagram making sure all leaves on Octagons point in same direction.

Border

Working around entire outer edge, join white with sl st in center sc of any 3-sc corner, ch 6, sl st in 3rd ch from hook, dc in same st, [◊skip next st, (dc, picot, dc) in next st, *skip next 2 sts, (dc, picot, dc) in next st; repeat from * 3 more times, skip next st◊, (dc, picot, dc) in next st]; repeat between [ ] around to last 15 sts; repeat between ◊◊, join with sl st in first sc, fasten off.

Assembly Diagram

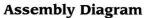

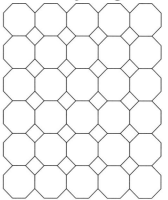

Holly Patch

Continued from page 132

sps. At end of last rnd, **do not** fasten off.

Rnd 10: Sl st in next st, ch 1; working left to right, **reverse sc** (see page 159) in same st, *ch 2, skip next st, (reverse sc in next st, ch 2, skip next st) around to next corner ch sp, (reverse sc, ch 2, reverse sc) in next ch sp; repeat from * 3 more times, ch 2, skip next st, (reverse sc in next st, ch 2, skip next st) around, join with sl st in first st, fasten off.

Square Assembly Diagram

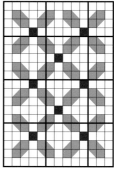

Rnd 10: Join black with sc in sp between 2 hcl on any corner shell, ch 7, sc in same sp, *[ch 4, skip next hcl, sc in top of next tr-cl, ch 4, skip next hcl, (sc in next st, ch 4, skip next hcl) 7 times, sc in top of next tr-cl, ch 4, skip next hcl], (sc, ch 7, sc) in sp between next 2 corner hcl; repeat from * 2 more times; repeat between [ ], join with sl st in first sc, fasten off.

Second Block

Rnds 1-9: Repeat same rnds of First Block (see page 135) reversing red and green.

Notes: *For **joining ch-7 sp,** ch 3, sc in 4th ch of corresponding ch-7 sp on other Block, ch 3.*

*For **joining ch-4 sp,** ch 2, sc in next ch-4 sp on other Block, ch 2.*

Rnd 10: Join black with sc in sp between 2 hcl on any corner shell; joining to side of last Block, joining ch-7 sp, sc in same sp on this Block, joining ch-4 sp, skip next hcl on this Block, sc in top of next tr-cl, joining ch-4 sp, skip next hcl on this Block, (sc in next st, joining ch-4 sp, skip next hcl on this Block) 7 times, sc in top of next tr-cl, joining ch-4 sp, skip next hcl on this Block, sc in sp between next 2 corner hcl, joining ch-7 sp, sc in same sp on this Block, *[ch 4, skip next hcl, sc in top of next tr-cl, ch 4, skip next hcl, (sc in next st, ch 4, skip next hcl) 7 times, sc in top of next tr-cl, ch 4, skip next hcl], (sc, ch 7, sc) in sp between next 2 corner hcl; repeat from*; repeat between [ ], join with sl st in first sc, fasten off.

Alternating colors on Blocks as shown in photo, repeat Second Block 2 more times for a total of 4 Blocks.

Second Row
First Block

Joining to bottom of First Row First Block, work same as First row Second Block.

Second Block

Rnds 1-9: Repeat same rnds of First Row First Block (see page 135).

Join black with sc in sp between 2 hcl on any corner shell; joining to bottom of next Block on last row, joining ch-7 sp, sc in same sp on this Block, *joining ch-4 sp, skip next hcl on this Block, sc in top of next tr-cl, joining ch-4 sp, skip next hcl on this Block, (sc in next st, joining ch-4 sp, skip next hcl on this Block) 7 times, sc in top of next tr-cl, joining ch-4 sp, skip next hcl on this Block, sc in sp between next 2 corner hcl, joining ch-7 sp, sc in same sp on this Block*; joining to side of last Block on this row; repeat between **, [ch 4, skip next hcl, sc in top of next tr-cl, ch 4, skip next hcl, (sc in next st, ch 4, skip next hcl) 7 times, sc in top of next tr-cl, ch 4, skip next hcl], (sc, ch 7, sc) in sp between next 2 corner hcl; repeat between [ ], join with sl st in first sc, fasten off.

Alternating colors on Blocks as shown, repeat Second Block 2 more times for a total of 4 Blocks,

Repeat Second Row 4 more times for a total of 6 rows.

Border

Rnd 1: Working around entire outer edge, join white with sc in any corner ch-7 sp, hcl, (sc in same lp, hcl) 2 times, *[(sc in next ch-4 sp or in next joining ch-7 sp, hcl) across] to next corner ch-7 sp, (sc, hcl) 3 times in next ch-7 sp; repeat from * 2 more times; repeat between [ ], join with sl st in first sc, fasten off.

Rnd 2: Join black with sc in any sc, ch 4, skip next hcl, (sc in next sc, ch 4, skip next hcl) around, join, fasten off. ✎

Candy Cane Throw

Designed by Margaret Elliff

Finished Size: 51" x 80".

Materials: Worsted-weight yarn — 30 oz. each red and white; P crochet hook or size needed to obtain gauge.

Gauge: 1 shell = 1¼" across; 1 shell = 1¼" tall.

Skill Level: ★★ Average

Afghan

Notes: Use 2 strands held together throughout.

*For **beginning diagonal shell**, (beg shell), ch 6, dc in 4th ch from hook, dc in each of last 2 chs.*

*For **diagonal shell (shell)**, (sl st, ch 3, 3 dc) around beg ch-3 of next shell.*

Row 1: With red, beg shell, turn (4 dc).

Row 2: Beg shell, shell, turn.

Rows 3-5: Beg shell, shell across, turn. At end of last row, fasten off.

Row 6: Join white with sl st in first st of first shell, beg shell, shell across, turn.

Rows 7-10: Beg shell, shell across, turn. At end of last row, fasten off.

Rows 11-15: With red, repeat rows 6-10.

Rows 16-35: Repeat rows 6-15 consecutively.

Row 36: Join white with sl st in ch-3 sp of first shell, ch 3, 3 dc in same sp, shell across, turn.

Row 37: Beg shell, shell across to last shell, sl st in top of ch-3 on last shell, turn.

*Note: For **decrease shell (dec shell)**, sl st in each of first 3 sts, sl st in next ch-3 sp, ch 3, 3 dc in same sp.*

Row 38: Dec shell, shell across, turn.

Rows 39-40: Repeat rows 37 and 38. At end of last row, fasten off.

Row 41: Join red with sl st in first st of first shell, beg shell, shell across to last shell, sl st in top of ch-3 on last shell, turn.

Rows 42-45: Repeat rows 38 and 37 alternately. At end of last row, fasten off.

Rows 46-55: Repeat rows 36-45.

Row 56: Repeat row 36.

Rows 57-60: Dec shell, shell across to last shell, sl st in top of ch-3 on last shell, turn. At end of last row, fasten off.

Row 61: Join red with sl st in ch-3 sp of first shell, ch 3, 3 dc in same sp, shell across to last shell, sl st in top of ch-3 on last shell, turn.

Rows 62-65: Repeat rows 57-60.

Row 66: With white, repeat row 61.

Rows 67-70: Repeat rows 57-60.

Rows 71-85: Repeat rows 61-70 consecutively, ending with row 65.

Row 86: With white, repeat row 61.

Rows 87-89: Repeat rows 57-59.

Row 90: Dec shell, sl st in top of ch-3 on last shell, fasten off.

Border

Rnd 1: Join white with sc in corner st; evenly spacing sts so piece lays flat, sc around outer edge, ending in multiples of 4, join with sl st in first sc.

Rnd 2: Sc in next st, 2 dc in next st, sc in next st, (sl st in next st, sc in next st, 2 dc in next st, sc in next st) around, join with sl st in joining sl st of last rnd, fasten off. ✍

Snowflake Hexagons

Designed by Maggie Weldon

Finished Size: 45" x 67½".

Materials: Worsted-weight yarn — 18 oz. each teal, berry and white; tapestry needle; I crochet hook or size needed to obtain gauge.

Gauge: Rnds 1-2 of Hexagon = 3¾" across. Each Hexagon is 7½" across from side to side and 8¼" across from point to point.

Skill Level: ★★ Average

Hexagon
(make 32 white/berry; make 28 white/teal)

Rnd 1: With white, ch 4, sl st in first ch to form ring, ch 2, 11 hdc in ring, join with sl st in top of ch-2 (12 hdc).

Note: For **picot,** ch 3, sl st in top of last st made.

Rnd 2: Ch 3, dc in same st, (tr, picot) in next st, *2 dc in next st, (tr, picot) in next st; repeat from * around, join with sl st in top of ch-3, fasten off (18 sts, 6 picots).

Note: For **front post fp,** (see page 159), yo, insert hook from front to back around post of next st on rnd before last, yo, draw lp through, (yo, draw through 2 lps on hook) 2 times. Skip next st on last rnd.

Rnd 3: Join color with sc in first st, *[fp around next st on rnd before last, skip next st on last rnd, sc in next st, ch 5, skip next picot], sc in next st; repeat from * 4 more times; repeat between [ ], join with sl st in first sc (12 sc, 6 fp, 6 ch sps).

Rnd 4: Ch 3, dc in each of next 2 sts, (2 dc, ch 1, 2 dc) in next ch sp, *dc in each of next 3 sts, (2 dc, ch 1, 2 dc) in next ch sp; repeat from * around, join with sl st in top of ch-3, fasten off (42 dc, 6 ch sps).

Rnd 5: Join white with sc in any ch sp, ch 3, sc in same sp, ch 3, skip next st, (sc in next st, ch 3, skip next st) 3 times,

*(sc, ch 3, sc) in next ch sp, ch 3, skip next st, (sc in next st, ch 3, skip next st) 3 times; repeat from * around, join with sl st in first sc, fasten off (30 ch sps).

Rnd 6: Join color with sl st in first corner ch sp, ch 3, (dc, ch 2, 2 dc) in same sp, 2 dc in each of next 4 ch sps, *(2 dc, ch 2, 2 dc) in next corner ch sp, 2 dc in each of next 4 ch sps; repeat from * around, join with sl st in top of ch-3, fasten off (12 dc across each side between corner ch sps).

Holding Hexagons wrong sides together, matching sts, sew together through **back lps** according to Assembly Diagram. ✎

Assembly Diagram

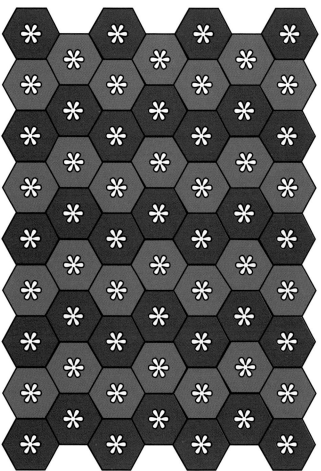

Christmas Tree Quilt

Designed by Martha Brooks Stein

Finished Size: 41" x 53½".

Materials: Worsted-weight yarn — 28½ oz. off-white, 8 oz. red and 4½ oz. green; tapestry needle; H and I crochet hooks or size needed to obtain gauge.

Gauge: With **I hook,** each Square = 2½" across.

Skill Level: ★★ Average

Solid Square
(make 208 off-white, 66 red and 14 green)

Rnd 1: With larger hook, ch 4, sl st in first ch to form ring, ch 3, 2 dc in ring, ch 2, (3 dc in ring, ch 2) 3 times, join with sl st in top of ch-3 (12 dc, 4 ch sps).

Rnd 2: Ch 3, dc in each st around with (2 dc, ch 2, 2 dc) in each ch sp, join, fasten off (28 dc, 4 ch sps).

Two–Color Square
(make 48)

Rnd 1: With larger hook and off-white, ch 4, sl st in first ch to form ring, ch 3, (2 dc, ch 2, 3 dc) in ring, ch 1 changing to green (see illustration), ch 1, (3 dc, ch 2, 3 dc) in ring, ch 1 changing to off-white, ch 1, join with sl st in top of ch-3.

Chain Color Change

Rnd 2: Ch 3, dc in each of next 2 sts, *2 dc, ch 2, 2 dc) in next ch sp, dc in each of next 3 sts, 2 dc in next ch sp*, ch 1 changing to green, ch 1, 2 dc in same ch sp as last 2 dc, dc in each of next 3 sts; repeat between **, ch 1 changing to off-white, ch 1, 2 dc in same ch sp, join, fasten off.

Holding Squares wrong sides together, matching sts, with matching color, sew together through **back lps** according to Square Assembly Diagram.

Border

Rnd 1: Working around entire outer edge in **back lps** only, with smaller hook and off-white, join with sc in first ch of corner ch sp before one short end, *[ch 2, sc in 2nd ch of same sp, sc in each st and sc in each ch sp on each side of seams across to next corner ch sp], sc in first ch of next corner ch sp; repeat from * 2 more times; repeat between [ ], join with sl st in first sc (144 sc across each short end between corner ch sps, 189 sc across each long edge between corner ch sps).

Rnd 2: Sl st in first ch sp, ch 1, sc in same sp, *(ch 2, skip next st, sc in next st) across to next corner ch sp, ch 2, sc in next corner ch sp, ch 2, sc in next st, (ch 2, skip next st, sc in next st) across to next corner ch sp, ch 2*, sc in next corner ch sp; repeat between **, join, fasten off. ✎

Square Assembly Diagram

Yuletide Ribbons

Designed by Hazel Osborn Jones

Finished Size: 52" x 72½".

Materials: Worsted-weight yarn — 52 oz. white and 9 oz. red/green/white variegated; H crochet hook or size needed to obtain gauge.

Gauge: 7 dc = 2"; 5 dc rows = 3".

Skill Level: ★ Easy

Afghan

Row 1: With white, ch 167, dc in 4th ch from hook, dc in each ch across, turn (165 dc).

Row 2: Ch 3, dc in next st, (ch 1, skip next st, dc in next st) across to last st, dc in last st, turn (84 dc, 81 ch sps).

Row 3: Ch 3, dc in next st, ch 1, skip next ch sp, (dc in next 19 sts and ch sps, ch 1, skip next ch sp) across to last 2 sts, dc in each of last 2 sts, turn (156 dc, 9 ch sps).

Rows 4-12: Ch 3, dc in next st, ch 1, skip next ch sp, (dc in next 19 sts, ch 1, skip next ch sp) across to last 2 sts, dc in each of last 2 sts, turn.

Row 13: Ch 3, dc in next st, ch 1, skip next ch sp, (dc in next st, ch 1, skip next st or ch sp) across to last 2 sts, dc in each of last 2 sts, turn.

Rows 14-113: Repeat rows 3-13 consecutively, ending with row 4. At end of last row, fasten off.

Ribbons

For each **horizontal ribbon** (make 11), with variegated, ch 195, sc in 2nd ch from hook, sc in each ch across, fasten off. Weave each horizontal ribbon through ch sps of rows 2, 13, 24, 35, 46, 57, 68, 79, 90, 101 and 112.

For each **vertical ribbon** (make 9), with variegated, ch 275, sc in 2nd ch from hook, sc in each ch across, fasten off. Weave each vertical ribbon from top to bottom through ch sps across Afghan.

Border

Rnd 1: Working around outer edge, with right side facing you, catching ends of each ribbon as you work, join white with sl st in corner st before one short end, ch 3, 2 dc in same st, dc in each st and 3 dc in end of each row around with 3 dc in each corner st, join with sl st in top of ch-3 (165 dc across each short end between corner dc, 341 dc across each long edge between corner dc).

Rnd 2: Ch 1, sc in first st, ch 6, skip next 3 sts, sc in next st, (ch 6, skip next 2 sts, sc in next st) around to last 3 sts, ch 6, skip last 3 sts, join with sl st in first sc (338 ch sps).

Rnd 3: Sl st in first ch sp, ch 4, 6 tr in same sp, sc in next ch sp, (7 tr in next ch sp, sc in next ch sp) around, join with sl st in top of ch-4, fasten off. ✐

Holiday Hearts

Designed by Tammy Hildebrand

Finished Size: 48" x 69½".

Materials: Fuzzy chunky yarn — 27 oz. off-white and 12 oz. burgundy; tapestry needle; J crochet hook or size needed to obtain gauge.

Gauge: 5 sts = 2"; 3 dc rows = 2". Each Block is 11½" x 13½".

Skill Level: ★★ Average

First Row
First Block

Row 1: With off-white, ch 17, dc in 4th ch from hook, dc in each ch across, turn (15 dc).

Note: *When changing colors (see page 159), always drop yarn to wrong side of work. Use a separate skein or ball of yarn for each color section.* **Do not** *carry yarn across from one section to another.*

Row 2: Ch 3, dc in next 5 sts changing to burgundy in last st made, dc in each of next 3 sts changing to off-white in last st made, dc in last 6 sts, turn.

Note: *Always change to next color in last st of last color used.*

Row 3: Ch 3, dc in next 4 sts; with burgundy, dc in next 5 sts; with off-white, dc in last 5 sts, turn.

Row 4: Ch 3, dc in each of next 3 sts; with burgundy, dc in next 7 sts; with off-white, dc in last 4 sts, turn.

Row 5: Ch 3, dc in each of next 2 sts; with burgundy, dc in next 9 sts; with off-white, dc in each of last 3 sts, turn.

Row 6: Ch 3, dc in next st; with burgundy, dc in next 11 sts; with off-white, dc in each of last 2 sts, turn.

Row 7: Ch 3; with burgundy, dc in next 13 sts; with off-white, dc in last st, turn.

Row 8: Ch 3; with burgundy, dc in next 6 sts, ch 1, skip next st, dc in next 6 sts; with off-white, dc in last st, turn.

Row 9: Ch 3, dc in next st; with burgundy, dc in next 4 sts; with off-white, dc in next st; working over next ch-1 sp, tr in skipped st on row before last, dc in next st on this row; with burgundy, dc in next 4 sts; with off-white, dc in each of last 2 sts, turn.

Row 10: Ch 3, dc in each of next 2 sts; with burgundy, dc in each of next 2 sts; with off-white, dc in next 5 sts; with burgundy, dc in each of next 2 sts; with off-white, dc in each of last 3 sts, turn. Fasten off burgundy.

Row 11: Ch 3, dc in each st across, **do not** turn.

Notes: *For* **beginning V-st (beg V-st),** *ch 5, dc in same st or sp.*

For **V-st,** *(dc, ch 2, dc) in next st or ch sp.*

Rnd 12: Working around outer edge, beg V-st, *ch 1, dc in end of same row, (ch 1, dc in end of next row) 10 times, ch 1*; working in starting ch on opposite side of row 1, V-st in first ch, ch 1, skip next ch, (dc in next ch, ch 1, skip next ch) 6 times, V-st in last ch; repeat between **; working in sts across last row, V-st in first st, ch 1, skip next st, (dc in next st, ch 1, skip next st) across, join with sl st in 3rd ch of ch-5.

Rnd 13: Sl st in first ch sp, beg V-st, *skip next dc of same V-st, (V-st in next st, skip next st) 6 times, V-st in ch sp of next V-st, V-st in each of next 7 ch-1 sps*, V-st in ch sp of next V-st; repeat between **, join (30 V-sts).

Rnd 14: Sl st in first ch sp, ch 3, (dc, ch 2, 2 dc) in same sp, *(V-st in next sp between V-sts) 7 times, (2 dc, ch 2, 2 dc) in next corner V-st, V-st in next 7 V-sts*, (2 dc, ch 2, 2 dc) in next corner V-st; repeat between **, join with sl st in top of ch-3.

Rnd 15: Sl st in next st, sl st in next ch sp, ch 2, (2 hdc, ch 2, 3 hdc) in same sp, *ch 1, 2 hdc in sp between next 2-dc group and next V-st, ch 1, (2 hdc in next sp between V-sts, ch 1) 6 times, 2 hdc in sp between next V-st and next 2-dc group, ch 1, (3 hdc, ch 2, 3 hdc) in next corner ch sp; ch 1, 2 hdc in sp between next 2-dc group and next V-st, ch 1, (2 hdc in next sp between V-sts, ch 1) 2 times, (sc in next sp between V-sts, ch 2) 2 times, (2 hdc in next sp between V-sts, ch 1) 2 times, 2 hdc in sp between next V-st and next 2-dc group, ch 1*, (3 hdc, ch 2, 3 hdc) in next corner ch sp; repeat between **, join with sl st in top of ch-2, fasten off.

Rnd 16: Join burgundy with sc in top right-hand corner ch sp, (sc, ch 2, 2 sc) in same sp, *ch 2, sl st in next ch-1 sp; working over ch sps of last rnd, (ch 1, 2 sc in next V-st on rnd before last) 3 times, ch 1, sl st in next V-st on rnd before last, (ch 1, 2 sc in next V-st on rnd before last) 3 times, ch 1, sl st in next ch-1 sp on last rnd, ch 2, (2 sc, ch 2, 2 sc) in next corner ch sp; working over ch sps of last rnd, ch 1, 3 hdc in sp between next 2 dc on rnd before last, (ch 1, 3 hdc in next V-st on rnd before last) 7 times, ch 1, 3 hdc in sp between next 2 dc on rnd before last, ch 1*, (2 sc, ch 2, 2 sc) in next corner ch sp; repeat between **, join with sl st in first sc, fasten off.

Rnd 17: Join off-white with sl st in first corner ch sp, ch 8, dc in same sp, (dc, ch 3, dc) in each ch sp around with (dc, ch 5, dc) in each corner ch sp, join with sl st in 3rd ch of ch-8, fasten off.

Second Block

Rows/Rnds 1-16: Repeat same rows/rnds of First Block (see page 149).

Rnd 17: Join off-white with sl st in first ch sp, ch 8, dc in same sp, (dc, ch 3, dc) in each ch sp across to next corner ch sp; joining to side of last Block, *dc in next corner ch sp, ch 2, drop lp from hook, insert hook in center ch of corresponding corner ch-5 sp on last Block, draw dropped lp through, ch 2, dc in same ch sp on this Block*, (dc in next ch sp, ch 1, drop lp from hook, insert hook in center ch of next ch-3 sp on last Block, draw dropped lp through, ch 1, dc in same ch sp on this Block) 10 times; repeat between **, (dc, ch 3, dc) in each ch sp

around with (dc, ch 5, dc) in corner ch sp, join with sl st in 3rd ch of ch-8, fasten off.

Repeat Second Block 2 more times for a total of 4 Blocks.

Second Row
First Block

Rows/Rnds 1-16: Repeat same rows/rnds of First Row First Block (see page 149).

Rnd 17: Join off-white with sl st in first ch sp; joining to bottom of First Block on last row, ch 5, drop lp from hook, insert hook in center joined ch of corresponding corner ch-5 sp on other Block, draw dropped lp through, ch 2, dc in same ch sp on this Block, (dc in next ch sp, ch 1, drop lp from hook, insert hook in center ch of next ch-3 sp on other Block, draw dropped lp through, ch 1, dc in same ch sp on this Block) 10 times, dc in next corner ch sp, ch 2, drop lp from hook, insert hook in center ch of next corner ch-5 sp on other Block, draw dropped lp through, ch 2, dc in same ch sp on this Block, (dc, ch 3, dc) in each ch sp around with (dc, ch 5, dc) in each corner ch sp, join with sl st in 3rd ch of ch-5, fasten off.

Second Block

Rows/Rnds 1-16: Repeat same rows/rnds of First Row First Block (see page 149).

Rnd 17: Join off-white with sl st in first ch sp; joining to bottom of next Block on last row, ch 5, drop lp from hook, insert hook in center ch of corresponding corner ch-5 sp on other Block, draw dropped lp through, ch 2, dc in same ch sp on this Block, *(dc in next ch sp, ch 1, drop lp from hook, insert hook in center ch of next ch-3 sp on other Block, draw dropped lp through, ch 1, dc in same ch sp on this Block) 10 times, dc in next corner ch sp, ch 2, drop lp from hook, insert hook in center ch of next corner ch-5 sp on other Block, draw dropped lp through, ch 2, dc in same ch sp on this Block*; joining to side of last Block on this row, repeat between **, (dc, ch 3, dc) in each ch sp around with (dc, ch 5, dc) in corner ch sp, join with sl st in 3rd ch of ch-5, fasten off.

Repeat Second Block 2 more times for a total of 4 Blocks.

Repeat Second Row 3 more times for a total of 5 rows.

Border

Rnd 1: Working over last rnd, join off-white with sl st in top right corner ch sp on rnd before last, ch 5, (tr, ch 1, tr, ch 1, tr, ch 1, tr) in same sp, work remainder of rnd according to Steps A–C:

Step A: *[Skip next sc on rnd before last, 2 dc in next sc, sc in each of next 2 V-sts on last rnd, (skip next sc on rnd before last, 4 dc in next sc, sc in each of next 2 V-sts on last rnd) 4 times, skip next sc on rnd before last, 2 dc in next sc], 7 dc around next joining sl st between Blocks; repeat from * 2 more times; repeat between [ ]; working over last rnd, tr in next corner ch sp on rnd before last, (ch 1, tr in same sp) 4 times;

Step B: *[Skip next sc on rnd before last, 3 dc in next sc, sl st in next V-st on last rnd, (3 dc in center st of next 3-dc group on rnd before last, sl st in next V-st on last rnd) 9 times, skip next sc on rnd before last, 3 dc in next sc], sl st in next joined ch-5 sp, 3 dc around next joining sl st between Blocks, sl st in next joined ch-5 sp; repeat from * 3 more times; repeat between [ ];

Step C: Working over last rnd, tr in next corner ch sp on rnd before last, (ch 1, tr in same sp) 4 times; repeat Step A; repeat Step B, join with sl st in 4th ch of ch-5, fasten off (141 sts across each short end between 5-tr corners, 59 3-dc groups across each long edge between 5-tr corners).

Rnd 2: Join burgundy with sl st in 2nd tr, [sc in next ch sp, ch 2, sc in next ch sp, sl st in next tr, ch 1, skip next tr, 2 sc in next st, (ch 1, skip next st, sc in next st) 14 times, *ch 2, skip next 4 sts, sl st in next st, ch 2, skip next 3 sts, sc in next st, (ch 1, skip next st, sc in next st) 14 times; repeat from * 2 more times, ch 1, sl st in 2nd tr of next 5-tr corner, sc in next ch sp, ch 2, sc in next ch sp, sl st in next tr, ch 1, (2 sc in 2nd st of next 3-dc group, ch 1) across] to next 5-tr corner, sl st in 2nd tr of next corner; repeat between [ ], join with sl st in first sl st, fasten off.

Heart Trim

Rnd 1: Working over top of Block, in off-white sts around outer edge of burgundy heart, join off-white with sc around post of dc before tr at center top of heart, sc around post of each of next 2 sts, ch 2, (sc around post of next st, ch 2) around, join with sl st in first sc, fasten off.

Rnd 2: Join burgundy with sl st in first st, sl st in each of next 2 sts, sc in next ch sp, sl st in next st, *(sc, ch 1, sc, ch 1, sc) in next ch sp, sl st in next st; repeat from * around to last ch sp, sc in last ch sp, join with sl st in first sl st, fasten off.

Repeat around heart of each Block.

Designed by Rosetta Harshman

Finished Size: 53½" x 63½".

Materials: Worsted-weight yarn — 38 oz. off-white, 15 oz. green, 6 oz. red; tapestry needle; G crochet hook or size needed to obtain gauge.

Gauge: 4 sc = 1"; 4 sc rows = 1". Each Block is 10¼" square.

Skill Level: ★★ Average

Block
(make 30)

Notes: For **beginning cluster (beg cl),** ch 3, (yo, insert hook in same sp, yo, draw lp through, yo, draw through 2 lps on hook) 2 times, yo, draw through all 3 lps on hook.

For **cluster (cl),** yo, insert hook in ring or next ch sp, yo, draw lp through, yo, draw through 2 lps on hook, (yo, insert hook in same sp, yo, draw lp through, yo, draw through 2 lps on hook) 2 times, yo, draw through all 4 lps on hook.

Rnd 1: With red, ch 8, sl st in first ch to form ring, beg cl in ring, ch 4, (cl in ring, ch 4) 7 times, join with sl st in top of first cl (8 cls).

Rnd 2: Sl st in next ch sp, beg cl, ch 5, sl st in 4th ch from hook, ch 1, cl in same sp, ch 3, (cl in next ch sp, ch 5, sl st in 4th ch from hook, ch 1, cl in same sp, ch 3) around, join, fasten off.

Rnd 3: Join green with sc in any ch-3 sp, ch 3, sc in same sp, ch 5, *(sc, ch 3, sc) in next ch-3 sp, ch 5; repeat from * around, join with sl st in first sc.

Rnd 4: Sl st in next ch sp, (ch 3, dc, ch 3, 2 dc) in same sp, ch 3, sc in next ch-5 sp, ch 3, *(2 dc, ch 3, 2 dc) in next ch sp, ch 3, sc in next ch-5 sp, ch 3; repeat from * around, join with sl st in top of ch-3.

Rnd 5: Ch 1, sc in each of first 2 sts, *[(2 sc, ch 3, 2 sc) in next ch sp, sc in each of next 2 sts, sc in next ch sp, ch 3, sc in next ch sp], sc in each of next 2 sts; repeat from * 6 more times; repeat between [ ], join with sl st in first sc, fasten off.

Rnd 6: Join off-white with sl st in last ch sp, (ch 3, 2 dc, ch 3, 3 dc) in same sp, *[ch 2; working behind rnd 5 between 2-dc groups on row before last, sc in next ch sp three rows below, ch 2], (3 dc, ch 3, 3 dc) in next ch sp on last row; repeat from * 6 more times; repeat between [ ], join with sl st in top of ch-3.

Notes: For **double treble crochet (dtr),** yo 3 times, insert hook in next st, yo, draw lp through, (yo, draw through 2 lps on hook) 4 times.

For **shell,** (sc, ch 2, sc) in next ch sp.

Rnd 7: Sl st in each of next 2 sts, sl st in next ch sp, ch 1, shell in same sp, *[ch 3, (dtr, ch 2, dtr, ch 2, dtr) in next sc, ch 3, skip next ch-2 sp], shell in next ch-3 sp; repeat from * 6 more times; repeat between [ ], join with sl st in first sc.

Rnd 8: Skipping dtr, ch 1, sc in each sc, 2 sc in each ch-2 sp and 3 sc in each ch-3 sp around with one sc in ch sp of each shell, join (104 sc).

Rnd 9: Ch 2, hdc in each st around, join with sl st in top of ch-2, fasten off.

Rnd 10: Join off-white with sl st in st above center st of any 3-dtr group 3 rows below; for **corner,** (ch 5, 2 dtr, ch 3, 3 dtr) in same st; *[dtr in next st, tr in next st, dc in each of next 2 sts, sc in next 17 sts, dc in each of next 2 sts, tr in next st, dtr in next st]; for **corner,** (3 dtr, ch 3, 3 dtr) in next st; repeat from * 2 more times; repeat between [ ], join with sl st in top of ch-5 (31 sts on each side between corner ch sps).

Rnd 11: Ch 2, hdc in each st around with (2 hdc, ch 2, 2 hdc) in each corner ch sp, join with sl st in top of ch-2 (35 hdc on each side between corner ch sps).

Rnd 12: Ch 3, skip next st, hdc in next st, ch 1, skip next st, hdc in next st, *(2 hdc, ch 3, 2 hdc) in next corner ch sp, hdc in next st, (ch 1, skip next st, hdc in next st) across to next corner ch sp; repeat from * 2 more times, (2 hdc, ch 3, 2 hdc) in next corner ch sp, (hdc in

Continued on page 155

Beaded Garlands

Designed by Maggie Weldon

Finished Size: 46" x 62" not including Fringe.

Materials: 100% wool 4-ply yarn — 46 oz. off-white, 3½ oz. each green, maroon, blue and violet; I crochet hook or size needed to obtain gauge.

Gauge: 7 dc = 2"; 2 dc rows = 1". 5 sets of pattern rows = 5½".

Skill Level: ★ Easy

Afghan

Notes: *Leave 6" end when joining or fastening off yarn.*

Front of row 1 is right side of work.

Row 1: With off-white, ch 219, dc in 4th ch from hook, dc in each ch across, turn (217 dc).

Rows 2-3: Ch 3, dc in each st across, turn. At end of last row, **do not** turn, fasten off.

Row 4: With right side facing you, join green with sc in first st, 3 sc in next st, (skip next 2 sts, 3 sc in next st) across to last 2 sts, skip next st, sc in last st, **do not** turn, fasten off (72 3-sc groups, 2 sc).

Row 5: With right side facing you, join off-white with sl st in first st, ch 3, dc in same st; (working over last row, 3 dc in 2nd skipped st on row before last) 71 times, 2 dc in last st on this row, turn (217 dc).

Row 6: Ch 3, dc in each st across, turn, fasten off.

Rows 7-126: Working row 4 in color sequence of maroon, blue, violet, green, repeat rows 4-6 consecutively. At end of last row, **do not** fasten off.

Row 127: Ch 3, dc in each st across, fasten off.

Fringe

For **each Fringe,** cut 4 strands yarn each 12" long. Holding all 4 strands together, fold in half, insert hook in end of row, draw fold through, draw all loose ends through fold including 6" ends, tighten. Trim ends.

Matching row color, Fringe in end of each row across short ends of Afghan. ✍

Santa's Bouquet

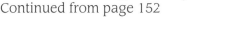

Continued from page 152

next st, ch 1, skip next st) across, join with sl st in 2nd ch of first ch-3, fasten off.

Holding Blocks wrong sides together, matching sts, with off-white, sew together through **back lps** in 5 rows of 6 Blocks each.

Border

Rnd 1: Working around outer edge, join off-white with sl st in ch sp before one short end, (ch 3, hdc, ch 1, hdc) in same sp, ◊*[ch 1, hdc in next st, ch 1, skip next st, hdc in next st, (ch 1, skip next ch sp, hdc in next st) 17 times, ch 1, skip next st, hdc in next st], ch 1, skip next ch sp, hdc in next seam*; repeat between ** 3 more times; repeat between [ ], ch 1, (hdc, ch 1, hdc, ch 1, hdc) in next corner ch sp; repeat between ** 5 times; repeat between [ ], ch 1◊, (hdc, ch 1, hdc, ch 1, hdc) in next corner ch sp; repeat between ◊◊, join with sl st in 2nd ch of ch-3, fasten off.

Rnd 2: Join red with sl st in any st, ch 3, (hdc in next st, ch 1) around, join as before, fasten off.

Rnd 3: Join green with sc in any ch sp, sc in same sp, ch 3, sl st in 3rd ch from hook, (2 sc in next ch sp, ch 3, sl st in 3rd ch from hook) around, join with sl st in first sc, fasten off. ✍

General Instructions

Yarn & Hooks

Always use the weight of yarn specified in the pattern so you can be assured of achieving the proper gauge. It is best to purchase at least one extra skein of each color needed to allow for differences in tension and dyes.

The hook size stated in the pattern is to be used as a guide. Always work a swatch of an afghan's stitch pattern with the suggested hook size. If you find your gauge is smaller or larger than what is specified, choose a different size hook.

Gauge

Gauge is measured by counting the number of rows or stitches per inch. Each of the afghans featured in this book will have a gauge listed. Gauge for some small motifs or flowers is given as an overall measurement. Proper gauge must be attained for the afghan to come out the size stated, and to prevent ruffling and puckering.

Make a swatch about 4" square in the stitch indicated in the gauge section of the instructions. Lay the swatch flat and measure the stitches. If you have more stitches per inch than specified in the pattern, your gauge is too tight and you need a larger hook. Fewer stitches per inch indicates a gauge that is too loose. In this case, choose a smaller hook size. Next, check the number of rows. If necessary, adjust your row gauge slightly by pulling the loops down a little tighter on your hook, or by pulling the loops up slightly to extend them.

Once you've attained the proper gauge, you're ready to start your afghan. Remember to check your gauge periodically to avoid problems later.

Pattern Repeat Symbols

Written crochet instructions typically include symbols such as parentheses, asterisks and brackets. In some patterns a diamond or bullet (dot), may be added.

( ) Parentheses enclose instructions which are to be worked again later or the number of times indicated after the parentheses. For example, "(2 dc in next st, skip next st) 5 times" means to follow the instructions within the parentheses a total of five times. If no number appears after the parentheses, you will be instructed when to repeat further into the pattern. Parentheses may also be used to enclose a group of stitches which

should be worked in one space or stitch. For example, "(2 dc, ch 2, 2 dc) in next st" means to work all the stitches within the parentheses in the next stitch.

* Asterisks may be used alone or in pairs, usually in combination with parentheses. If used in pairs, the instructions enclosed within asterisks will be followed by instructions for repeating. These repeat instructions may appear later in the pattern or immediately after the last asterisk. For example, "*Dc in next 4 sts, (2 dc, ch 2, 2 dc) in corner sp*, dc in next 4 sts; repeat between ** 2 more times" means to work through the instructions up to the word "repeat," then repeat only the instructions that are enclosed within the asterisks twice.

If used alone an asterisk marks the beginning of instructions which are to be repeated. Work through the instructions from the beginning, then repeat only the portion after the * up to the word "repeat"; then follow any remaining instructions. If a number of times is given, work through the instructions one time, repeat the number of times stated, then follow the remainder of the instructions.

[ ] Brackets, ◊ diamonds and • bullets are used in the same manner as asterisks. Follow the specific instructions given when repeating.

Finishing

Patterns that require assembly will suggest a tapestry needle in the materials. This should be a #16 or #18 blunt-tipped tapestry needle. When stitching pieces together, be careful to keep the seams flat so pieces do not pucker.

Hiding loose ends is never a fun task, but if done correctly, will keep your afghan looking great for years. Always leave 6-8" of yarn when beginning or ending. Thread the loose end into your tapestry needle and carefully weave through the back of several stitches. Then, weave in the opposite direction, going through different strands. Gently pull the end and clip, allowing the end to pull up under the stitches.

If your afghan needs blocking, a light steam pressing works well. Lay your afghan on a large table or on the floor, shaping and smoothing by hand as much as possible. Adjust your steam iron to the permanent press setting, then hold slightly above the stitches, allowing the steam to penetrate the yarn. Do not rest the iron on the afghan. Allow to dry completely.

Skill Level Requirements:

★ *Easy* — Requires knowledge of basic skills only; great for beginners or anyone who wants quick results.

★ ★ *Average* — Requires some experience; very comfortable for accomplished stitchers, yet suitable for beginners wishing to expand their abilities.

★ ★ ★ *Advanced* — Requires a high level of skill in all areas; average stitchers may find some areas of these patterns difficult, though still workable.

★ ★ ★ ★ *Challenging* — Requires advanced skills in both technique and comprehension, as well as a daring spirit; some areas may present difficulty for even the most accomplished stitchers.

For More Information

Sometimes even the most experienced needlecrafters can find themselves having trouble following instructions. If you have difficulty completing your project, write to:

Afghan Sentiments Editors
The Needlecraft Shop
23 Old Pecan Road
Big Sandy, Texas 75755

Acknowledgments

Yarn Companies

Caron International:
All-American Cats . . . . Wintuk
Christmas Tree Quilt . . Dawn Sayelle & Wintuk
Forget-Me-Not . . . . Dazzleaire
Hexagon Floral . . . . Dawn Sayelle
Holly Patch . . . . Simply Soft
Lush Delights . . . . Dazzleaire
Pink Rosebuds . . . . Wintuk
Shells In Song . . . . Kolor Match
Snowflake Hexagons . . . . Dazzleaire
Triangle Treasure . . . . Dawn Sayelle
Victorian Poinsettia . . . . Wintuk

Coats & Clark:
Candy Cane Throw . . . . . Red Heart Super Saver
Clematis . . . . Red Heart Classic
E Pluribus Unum . . . . Red Heart Fleck
Evergreen Classic . . . . . . Red Heart Super Saver
Gentle Serenade . . . . Red Heart Super Saver
Greek Silhouette . . . . . . Red Heart Super Saver
Hearts A' Flight . . . . Paton's Decor
Indian Summer . . . . Paton's Canadiana
Marbled Elegance . . . . . Red Heart Super Saver
Milady's Lace . . . . South Maid Cotton 8
Native Colors . . . . Red Heart With Wool
Painted Daisy . . . . Paton's Canadiana
Rose Trellis . . . . Paton's Decor
Shining Stars . . . . Red Heart Jeweltones
Soothing Lullaby . . . . . . Red Heart Super Saver
Square Dance . . . . Red Heart Classic
Thunderbird . . . . Red Heart Super Saver
Tulip Field . . . . Red Heart With Wool
Tulips In Bloom . . . . Red Heart Classic
White on White . . . . Red Heart Super Saver

Lion Brand:
Cool Water . . . . Jiffy
Holiday Hearts . . . . Jiffy
Twilight Trails . . . . Jiffy

Watercolor Plaid . . . . Jiffy

Spinrite:
American Star . . . . Bernat Berella "4"
Beaded Garland . . . . Muskoka
Gothic Romance . . . . Bernat Berella "4"
Lavender Echoes . . . . Bernat Berella "4"
Lyrical Waves . . . . Bernat Berella "4"
Rose In Lace . . . . Bernat Berella "4"
Rustic Cabins . . . . Bernat Berella "4"

Stitching Artists

Shirley Brown . . . . Floral Tiles
Susie Spier-Maxfield . . . . E Pluribus Unum

Photography

East Texas Homes & Locations:
Robin & Kepen Gilliam, Frankie Sherman—Arp; Rochelle Boyce—Gladewater; Mike & Beth Augustine—Longview; Ruth & Glynn Mitchell—Mineola; Judy & Bill Hammonds, Harrel & Mataline Broach, Dana & Marianne Havron, Tankersley Garden—Mt. Pleasant; Terry & Jill Waggoner—Overton; Bill & Ruth Whitaker—Tyler

Models:
Nathan Chaffin; Robin, Seth & Ely Gilliam; Greg, Cheryl & Casey Moore; Thomas, Bonne & Savannah Reed; Donna Robertson; Fran Rohus; Jill, Hannah & Savannah Waggoner

Cover Model:
Jana Robertson

Special Help With Props:
Allens Nursery; Big Sandy High School Music Department; Country Girl Antiques & Dana Taylor; Loren Edelbach; Sandy Kennebeck; Mundt Music

Stitch Guide

Standard Stitch Abbreviations

ch(s)	chain(s)
dc	double crochet
dtr	double treble crochet
hdc	half double crochet
lp(s)	loop(s)
rnd(s)	round(s)
sc	single crochet
sl st	slip stitch
sp(s)	space(s)
st(s)	stitch(es)
tog	together
tr	treble crochet
tr tr	triple treble crochet
yo	yarn over

Single Crochet (sc)

Insert hook in st (a), yo, draw lp through, yo, draw through both lps on hook (b).

Half Double Crochet (hdc)

Yo, insert hook in st (a), yo, draw lp through (b), yo, draw through all 3 lps on hook (c).

Front Loop (a)/Back Loop (b)
(front lp/back lp)

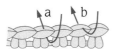

Chain (ch)

Yo, draw hook through lp.

Slip Stitch (sl st)

Insert hook in st, yo, draw through st and lp on hook.

Double Crochet (dc)

Yo, insert hook in st (a), yo, draw lp through (b), (yo, draw through 2 lps on hook) 2 times (c and d).

The patterns in this book are written using American crochet stitch terminology. For our international customers, hook sizes, stitches and yarn definitions should be converted as follows:			But, as with all patterns, test your gauge (tension) to be sure.

US	= UK	Thread/Yarns		Crochet Hooks			
sl st (slip stitch)	= sc (single crochet)	Bedspread Weight = No.10 Cotton or Virtuoso		Metric	US	Metric	US
sc (single crochet)	= dc (double crochet)	Sport Weight = 4 Ply or thin DK		.60mm	14	3.00mm	D/3
hdc (half double crochet)	= htr (half treble crochet)	Worsted Weight = Thick DK or Aran		.75mm	12	3.50mm	E/4
dc (double crochet)	= tr (treble crochet)			1.00mm	10	4.00mm	F/5
tr (treble crochet)	= dtr (double treble crochet)	Measurements		1.50mm	6	4.50mm	G/6
dtr (double treble crochet)	= ttr (triple treble crochet)	1" = 2.54 cm		1.75mm	5	5.00mm	H/8
skip	= miss	1 yd. = .9144 m		2.00mm	B/1	5.50mm	I/9
		1 oz. = 28.35 g		2.50mm	C/2	6.00mm	J/10

Treble Crochet *(tr)*

Yo 2 times, insert hook in st (a), yo, draw lp through (b), (yo, draw through 2 lps on hook) 3 times (c, d and e).

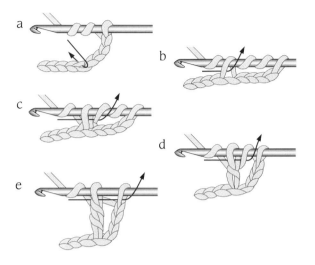

Double Treble Crochet *(dtr)*

Yo 3 times, insert hook in st (a), yo, draw lp through (b), (yo, draw through 2 lps on hook) 4 times (c, d, e and f).

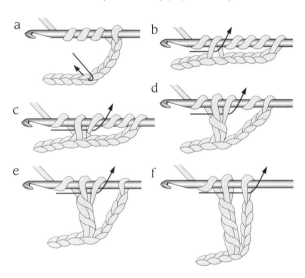

Front Post/Back Post Stitches *(fp/bp)*

Yo, insert hook from front to back (a) or back to front (b) around post of st on indicated row; complete as stated in pattern.

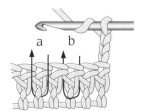

Reverse Single Crochet *(reverse sc)*

Working from left to right, insert hook in next st to the right (a), yo, draw through st, complete as sc (b).

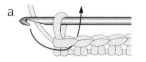 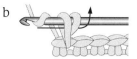

Single Crochet Color Change
(sc color change)

Drop first color; yo with 2nd color, draw through last 2 lps of st.

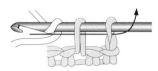

Double Crochet Color Change
(dc color change)

Drop first color; yo with 2nd color, draw through last 2 lps of st.

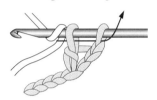

Single Crochet next 2 stitches together
(sc next 2 sts tog)

Draw up lp in each of next 2 sts, yo, draw through all 3 lps on hook.

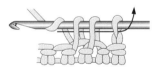

Half Double Crochet next 2 stitches together *(hdc next 2 sts tog)*

(Yo, insert hook in next st, yo, draw lp through) 2 times, yo, draw through all 5 lps on hook.

Double Crochet next 2 stitches together
(dc next 2 sts tog)

(Yo, insert hook in next st, yo, draw lp through, yo, draw through 2 lps on hook) 2 times, yo, draw through all 3 lps on hook.

Index

Designers